GET THE JOB!

INTERVIEW STRATEGIES THAT WORK

MARILYN PINCUS

Illustrations by Deborah Zemke

MJF BOOKS
New York

DEDICATION

THIS BOOK IS DEDICATED TO
THE MEMORY OF BURTON PINCUS.
APRIL 27, 1936–OCTOBER 9, 1997
GONE TOO SOON, BUT REMEMBERED EVERY DAY
BY SOMEONE WHO LOVED HIM.

Published by MJF Books
Fine Communications
322 Eighth Avenue
New York, NY 10001

Get the Job!
LC Control Number: 2010922864
ISBN-13: 978-1-60671-019-7
ISBN-10: 1-60671-019-2

Previously published as *Interview Strategies That Lead to Job Offers*

This revised, updated, and retitled edition is published by MJF Books in
arrangement with Barron's Educational Press, Inc.

Copyright © 1999, 2010 by Barron's Educational Series, Inc.

Printed in the United States of America.

MJF Books and the MJF colophon are trademarks of Fine Creative Media, Inc.

WCM   10   9   8   7   6   5   4   3   2   1

Contents

Introduction

◆

HOW YOU + THEY BECOME US

It's easy to become narrowly focused when you're faced with the task of getting a job offer. You think of what you need and want. This is not the time for distractions. You probably long to restore yourself to a "normal" life. Job searches are stressful! Before you plunge headlong into your job quest, however, take a moment to examine the bigger picture.

Focus on the potential employer's wants and needs.

Find a way to fill the need—convince the employer you can do so and you'll receive the job offer.

SALES, SALES, SALES!

◆ A job interview is a sales meeting.

◆ Star salespeople deliver benefits.

◆ They talk to a prospect about the sizzle when they're attempting to sell the steak.

◆ They rely on the dictum that words tell but stories sell.

◆ No matter what job title you desire, when you're being interviewed you're a salesperson.

CLOSE EARLY, CLOSE OFTEN

1. Plan to feature a few key benefits when you meet with interviewers—attributes you'll bring to the job that will meet the
employer's wants and needs.

2. Case closed.

3. If an interviewer raises another question, discuss additional
attributes that relate directly to the interviewer's probe.

4. Case closed.

In other words, stay focused and sell. Don't say more than is necessary. Successful salespeople know it's essential to recognize when
the sale has been made.

Get the Job! Interview Strategies That Work guides you through
the process. It's a veritable instruction manual incorporating the
most successful sales techniques into interview strategies so you can
automatically perform like an ace salesperson. Even when you're
selecting an interview outfit, tips and techniques will focus on that
interview outfit as it relates to selling yourself—making a dynamite
appearance when you arrive for the interview.

PERSONAL STYLE

Some very successful salespeople are quiet; others are loud, quick
to shake hands and tell a joke. *Get the Job! Interview Strategies
That Work* acknowledges that people are different. As you adapt
tips and techniques you'll use to sell yourself, you'll be given the
opportunity to make choices that permit you to complement your
personal style and support your comfort level.

Chapter 4 spotlights a phenomenon referred to as *mirroring*. The way you position your arms and legs, lean forward or backward, and arrange yourself to reflect the interviewer's physical position influences the interviewer's assessment of you. Once you understand how mirroring works, right down to the management of your vocal pitch and pace, you're able to use it to your advantage.

The way you approach interviewers will depend upon how much you know about their communication style. Read about this in Chapter 3 where Predictable Questions are discussed. A clear desk and orderly office, for example, could send a message to the tuned-in observer that this individual is likely to be what Dr. William Marston, a psychologist at Columbia University, refers to as a High C person.

A High C person is generally cautious and tentative in decision making. That person will be prepared for your arrival, will have read your job application or letters of recommendation, and will have precise and detailed questions ready to ask. Marston, who developed a system for identifying behavior and communication models, concludes that it's better that you not generalize when you answer High C people. Precise and detailed responses will make them comfortable. On the other hand, many interviewers today use *virtual offices*. You may not be able to assess a communication style by observing physical surroundings and shouldn't make that mistake.

Get the Job! Interview Strategies That Work holds up a No Admittance sign to extraneous information. At the same time, nothing significant is left out. This valuable, easy-to-carry-anywhere, easy-to-read volume is packed with the information you need to move

from job seeker status to new employee. It tells the story of how You + They Become Us.

Make this story your own.

ACKNOWLEDGMENT
A special thanks to Ms. Max Reed, Senior Editor at Barron's, who slipped into the driver's seat after the original manuscript was delivered, and drove it to the end of the line—Bookdom.

Chapter 1

Treat Every Interview Like an Important Interview

"Be better prepared than you think you will need to be."

—H. Jackson Brown, Jr.

There is a Dutch proverb that proclaims: "He who is outside the door has already a good part of his journey behind him." Well, congratulate yourself—you got yourself invited in for a show-and-tell session. That's not a minor achievement; however, you want a job offer. That means that a good part of the journey begins *now*. The job offer should go to the person who demonstrates he or she can perform a specific job better than the competition.

You're selling a product and the product is YOU.

Successful salespeople feel good about the product they sell.

YOUR CHIEF OBJECTIVE

All this is of no importance if you don't feel outrageously positive about wanting the job.

Make the job for which you're interviewing your chief objective.

Everything else discussed in this book is secondary to this simple observation.

Successful people are enthusiastic about what they do. It's difficult to be enthusiastic and sincere about your enthusiasm when you're unsure about what you want. You can read more about this in Chapter 13, A Powerful Strategy That Guarantees Success.

So, you've arrived at the door. You're determined to succeed and enthusiastic about getting the job offer. Can you demonstrate this to the interviewer(s)? Absolutely!

STRATEGIES TO REMEMBER

1. Arrive on time, smile, maintain an erect posture, use a firm handshake (all to be discussed in greater detail in Chapter 4, It Takes More Than New Clothes to Help You Look Good).

2. *Fit in.* Here's a key point job seekers should consider. The hiring process is costly and most employers don't want to rehire. When everything else *fits* (such as educational background, job experience), the people making the hiring decisions want to know you'll be happy. If you're content, you're more likely to make a smooth transition; you'll make it easy for other employees to welcome you and work with you and you'll stay with the company.

3. *Compliment the company.* "Why do you want to work here?" is a frequently asked question. If no one asks, let the interviewer

know, anyway: "I want to work for a fine company." "I want to work with people who have high standards." "The ABC Company brings excellent products to the marketplace. It would make me feel good to know I contribute to the process."

4. *Listen carefully.* "The interviewer is a valuable person who has something valuable to say," is the message you send when you listen carefully. Interviewers are only human; they should feel good about the message you send. That impacts favorably on their assessment of you. It also suggests you listen carefully to others and quickly grasp what's expected of you. A good way to demonstrate you're listening is to repeat the interviewer's phrases when you speak.

◆ "It's good to know people in this department are on the same page." "I agree that clear communication makes it easier to accomplish tasks."

◆ "It's refreshing to hear you say that the company is trying to do better. A giant like XYZ is already a winner; people might think you don't need to try to do better."

5. *Think before you speak.* An excellent interviewer makes you feel comfortable. A job candidate who feels comfortable is inclined to speak more easily; still, you want to guard against saying too much.

"I look forward to having a good income and benefits if I join this company," may be accurate and even complimentary, but, "I need the money" kind of comments are best left unsaid. Don't be so relaxed that you say, "I know I shouldn't say this, but . . ." If you shouldn't say it—don't!

Even when there's good chemistry between you and the interviewer, think before you speak. Except for the usual small talk—comments about the weather or observations about how easy it was to travel to this rural office setting—your words should be measured. Avoid shooting from the hip and you won't make statements that can boomerang.

6. *Do something memorable.* If you can think of a way to set yourself apart from other job candidates, you may enhance your front-runner position; for example, if you're interviewing for a position in marketing, bring along a company advertisement. Can you give specific reasons why this advertisement is terrific? This can be risky since the interviewer may disagree with your assessment. On the other hand, your evaluation can win favor. Even if the interviewer doesn't agree with you, he or she may

appreciate your skill in offering an intelligent assessment and showing initiative.

7. *Make substitutions to satisfy needs.* If the employer is looking for someone with management experience and you can't point to a job history of management experience, it's possible you've had this experience in another venue. A five-year stint as stage manager at the local community theater, for example, qualifies as management experience. If possible, inject this information into the conversation with a story. Stories sell!

A job candidate who was a theater stage manager relates an amusing story about something that came up unexpectedly, which spotlights how he *managed*.

"One night the leading man brought his dog to the theater. The dog heard his owner's voice rising in distress during a staged argument and somehow the dog slipped out of the dressing room and bolted onto the stage to investigate. I added a meat loaf sandwich to my arsenal of management tools that night! The dog was enticed off stage in record time."

8. *Plan your exit remarks.* Great exit "scripts" help you maintain your good image as the interview winds down. You'll move purposely as you exit and avoid having should've said, could've said second thoughts after you leave.

◆ "The company's state-of-the-art warehouse is impressive. I like what I see and would like to be a part of future success. Thanks for showing me around."

◆ "Tucson is an exciting city. My family and I would be very happy here. We'll both be waiting to hear management's hiring decision. Thanks again for your time."

◆ I knew a lot about the Bronson Company before I arrived and am eager to work here. After what you and Mr. Smith told me about the marketing campaign planned for The Netherlands, I'm going to find it difficult to await your hiring decision—I want to be where the action is!"

Admittedly, it would be difficult to preplan these remarks. They're based on specific information that came to light during the interview. Nevertheless, you can plan the gist of the remark in advance and fill it in when the time comes. Specific references to the company and what transpired during the interview make the exit lines strong. When you know you'll say something about company facilities, company plans, moving to a new city for a new job, and so on, you're better prepared.

If you prefer, say something generic. Your goal is to make a graceful exit while keeping the energy level up.

BE HAPPY

Several years ago a popular song urged "Don't worry. Be happy."

You want to make others happy. If you're thinking about your next mortgage payment and your dwindling checking account balance, it's difficult to be happy and enthusiastic, so, if you have problems that cause you worry, work to remedy them. Your bank account can be boosted, for example, by signing on with a temporary agency and accepting part-time assignments while job hunting. If your car is not dependable, perhaps you can take public transportation to job interviews. Look for creative approaches to remedy things that make you unhappy and be happy! Your smiles and good humor will help you win favor.

DIRECTED DAYDREAMING

Golf legend Jack Nicklaus is one accomplished individual who reportedly visualizes or "sees" his performance before it happens. It's not a new idea and you may have read or heard about it before. Creative visualization, directed daydreaming, imagery rehearsal—they're all the same thing. Sports psychologists coach athletes who want to perfect this approach to relaxing and staging a winning performance.

You can use it to restore energy and reach your goals, too. On the elevator ride up to the interview, as you sit in the waiting room or, when you're asked to fill out an application before the interview, take a few moments to focus on breathing in and out. This helps clear your mind. Then, see yourself seated across from the interviewer and responding to the question: "When can you start?"

An article in the Mind and Body section of the magazine, *Chatelaine* (May 1996) suggests that a mental preview sets you up for performing with a positive attitude. You've already *experienced* success and know what it feels like, so you're better prepared to go through the motions that get you to the end result.

In any event, like eating a bowl of chicken soup when you have a cold or the flu, it can't hurt. If you want to explore or perfect this technique, check with sports psychologists practicing nearby. Classes may be offered at health spas, local community centers, or you can arrange for a few private sessions. Mastering this strategy may turn out to be a great way to boost your confidence level and help you enjoy a calmer approach to every challenge you face.

No doubt about it, getting a job offer is a challenge. But, you're going to get offers and get them faster when you put all the odds in your favor.

Fit in and you'll be invited in!

Chapter 2

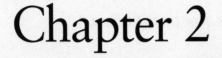

Do You Sound Like Your Résumé?

◆

"Honesty's the best policy."

—Cervantes

UPDATE YOUR RESUME

A résumé reports what you've done as it relates to what you can do for the potential employer. What you say about your background and experience during an interview and what you write should be in harmony or you undermine your credibility.

Faith, confidence, reliance, and trust are qualities an employer hopes to find in a new employee.

Assuming some time has passed since you generated your résumé, and that you submitted it prior to your interview date, read it before you keep the appointment. Are you ready to back up what you wrote? If someone else prepared your résumé, does it accurately state your case?

If you're planning to submit your résumé when you arrive, be ready to demonstrate that what's in print represents you and what you can deliver.

DELIVER WHAT YOU PROMISE

Use the following exercise to examine the merit of this advice.

1. Marge G.'s résumé states she operates a popular spreadsheet program. During the interview, however, she explains the program is on her home computer but she doesn't use it. She says, "I'm ready to teach myself how to use it. It's available to me. This will be easy to do."

   You're the interviewer. Which statement is most accurate?

   ◆ Marge can't operate the spreadsheet program. Her résumé reported she could.

   ◆ Marge is anxious to please. She'll learn the spreadsheet program.

2. Jane R.'s résumé boasts she teaches courses at the local community college in how to use spreadsheets. She tells the interviewer, "I teach a course on how to deal with difficult coworkers, too."

   You're the interviewer. Which statement is most accurate?

   ◆ Jane R. has excellent spreadsheet skills.

   ◆ She has skills that would prepare her for getting along with our internal and external customers.

3. Mark P.'s résumé states he was a warehouse assistant in a 60,000-square-foot warehouse. When the XYZ warehouse foreman interviews him, Mark explains, "It was my uncle's warehouse and I only worked on weekends when big shipments were scheduled

to arrive and he couldn't get his regular crew to work. I can operate a forklift."

You're the foreman. Which statement is most accurate?

◆ Mark has limited hands-on warehouse experience.

◆ Mark wasted my time. I advertised for an experienced warehouse assistant.

EXAGGERATION VERSUS CREDIBILITY

Marge was dishonest. Jane probably delighted the interviewer by
showing she could deliver more than was expected. Was Mark dishonest or did he exaggerate? More importantly, how would the
interviewer answer this question?

"Honesty Counts In Job Interviews," is the title of an article in the
Personal Futures section of the July/August 1997 issue of *The
Futurist*. The title, alone, is a worthwhile directive and the information it contains spotlights a modern phenomenon. Concerns
about legal ramifications make people reluctant to provide comprehensive references for job candidates. As a result, ". . . interviewers are scrutinizing the character and candor of candidates
more carefully."

> *"Forget trying to smooth-talk your way through
> your next job interview. Just be sure you mean
> what you say."*
>
> *That's the advice of Robert Half International, a
> staffing services firm, which polled 150 hiring
> executives from 1,000 U.S. companies on what
> they look for in job candidates. Nearly one-third*

of the executives rated honesty and integrity as the most critical qualities in a job candidate, up from 7 percent in 1990 when verbal skills ranked number one.

If Mark's interviewer is one of the 150 hiring executives polled, there's a better than 30 percent chance he would label Mark dishonest.

Unofficial inquiry in offices around the country suggest, however, that not everyone who has a great job today subscribed 100 percent of the time to the advice to be honest. You probably know at least one young and inexperienced job seeker who said he had job experience when he didn't. He was hired. He was fired. Hired. Fired. Eventually, he truly had job experience!

If you're looking for a perfect guideline, you know you won't find it. On the other hand, research suggests that the price you pay for inconsistency or dishonesty is high. If you misrepresent your experience and skills, you may be hired to perform as someone you're not. In the long run, nothing good is likely to result. It's the *be careful what you wish for, you might get it* scenario in action.

RESUME FRAUD

Have you heard the one about the man who wanted someone to pay for airline tickets when he traveled to beautiful places? He perfected a résumé designed to attract a hospital position and responded to employment advertisements at hospitals located in cities he wanted to visit. Potential employers provided airfare. Actually, he didn't want a job; he wanted to minimize the cost of a vacation. His fraudulent résumé doubled as his ticket to ride!

Then there's the one about the young man who was one semester shy of earning his college degree. He was hired and later fired. He didn't need a college degree for the job but when the employer learned he lied about having a degree, he dismissed him.

Stories regarding serious résumé fraud are easy to find. Honesty tests administered to job applicants at some companies were designed largely as a response to this kind of abuse.

It bears mentioning that potential employers have probably seen it all. You need only look at articles in resources like *Workforce Management* (www.workforce.com), such as the one entitled "Résumé Fraud: Lies, Omissions, and Exaggerations" to know Human Resources professionals are forewarned.

Workplace crime expert Jane Y. Kusic, mentioned in *Nation's Business* (April 1, 1997), is owner and president of White Collar Crime 101, based in McLean, Virginia. Ms. Kusic points out that risk is minimized when an employer hires honest people.

It really shouldn't require an expert to remind us that honesty is a prized quality. However, it's an important message to impart.

YOUR PERSONALITY'S SHOWING

A résumé has a personality.

◆ Is it without frills and to the point?

◆ Is it cluttered with a stilted vocabulary?

◆ Does it talk much, say little?

◆ Is it detailed and complete?

◆ Is it clear and easy to read?

Does your résumé reflect your personality? If you have a résumé with no frills that's to the point, but you tend to be detailed and complete when you speak, you may be raising a red flag.

A résumé that is meant to help introduce you can't do a good job if it doesn't reflect your personality.

Sean K. got help organizing his thoughts and writing his résumé. He applied at five different sporting goods supply stores for an assistant manager position. When he spoke with the interviewer at the largest store, she asked him to write a new résumé.

"This job requires good writing skills. A résumé is a writing sample, but I need to see one you wrote yourself. Formula résumés don't count."

Marla T. was concerned about having to account for six months off when she had a nervous breakdown. Although the résumé service she used was able to include that period and explain it without fanfare, many of the words the service used were pretentious.

"We need someone with excellent command of the English language, Ms. T. We were impressed with your use of language when we read your résumé," Marla was told.

"I don't never want to miss out on a good learning opportunity," she commented when told job candidates attend a four-week training program prior to being hired. The company may or may not extend a job offer at the end of that time.

Although Marla attended the training program, it was soon obvious she never *sounded* like her résumé. She wasn't the person for the job and wasn't hired.

Tish Branning hired accountants for her firm's worldwide operations. She was accustomed to seeing their detailed and complete résumés. "That's what an accountant is like," she observed, "detailed and complete."

Bev Ireland almost missed being interviewed because her résumé was lean and Tish Branning put it to one side and almost didn't call. During the interview, however, Bev gave detailed and well-rounded responses to questions. She didn't *sound* like her résumé and that worked in her favor; she was hired. Still, her résumé was not the asset it could have been.

◆

CHOOSE YOUR WORDS STRATEGICALLY

Joyce Lain Kennedy in *Resumes for Dummies* (Wiley Publishing, Inc., 5th edition, 2007), assigns lists of "Wow Words" to job-specific areas.

◆ *Critiqued and revitalized* are among the many words you can slip into résumés if you're searching for communications and creativity positions.

◆ *Reconstructed and systematized* are some of the dozens of verbs Ms. Kennedy highlights for use by those seeking technical positions.

She offers ten key areas of word recommendations and tells how "power-play" verbs *campaign* for you. You're alerted to avoid using the same word twice. (Reach for that thesaurus without hesitation!) Kennedy points to keywords you'd want to include in electronic résumés. (Writers can get sappy on the subject of words and, lest I get carried away, let me mention this writer finds Ms. Kennedy's book about résumé preparation easy to read, upbeat and *valuable*, a most important word! Moreover, this latest edition is definitely in step with the times.)

WORDS, WORDS, WORDS

The words you choose help you, through your résumé, to sound *good* or *not so good*.

1. Scan your résumé for action words. Try to double the number now in use. In the unlikely event you don't find any verbs, add at least six (an arbitrary number, but it helps set a goal).

2. Be stingy. Use fewer rather than more words.

3. Avoid abbreviations and industry jargon that may not be widely understood.

4. "Short words are best and old words when short are best of all"—attributed to Sir Winston Spencer Churchill. You can think of it this way: Use words most people will understand.

5. Spell accurately. A computerized spelling check won't catch all errors. If, for example, you misspell a company name and the computer "flags" the name, it's tempting for you to move on because you assume the name is properly spelled. Take time to confirm accuracy.

6. Use words that say what you mean. Although you say what you mean when speaking aloud, you may not write what you mean; for instance,

> *"Authority for making final decisions."*

This is an impressive claim. Can you back it up? If you were, in fact, a team member who shared the task of making final decisions, say so.

> *"Shared responsibility for making final decisions."*

The word *responsibility* replaced the word *authority*. The word *shared* was added, and *voilà*—it's a-say-what-you-mean addition to the résumé. Moreover, it's an impressive claim and you can confirm it rather than backslide if the interviewer wants to explore it further.

If you want to explore this subject further, read Ms. Kennedy's *Resumes for Dummies* and other fine books that will guide you through the résumé-writing process.

Remember, a résumé that works for you

◆ helps you get an interview.

◆ acts as a launchpad permitting you to expand on what you delivered in the résumé.

◆ impresses all the vital players from Human Resource professional to manager who will work with you if you're hired.

Finally, it permits you to properly represent yourself so you're likely to be offered a job you can do and will enjoy doing.

Chapter 3

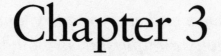

What You Know About a Company Pays Off

"Every science and every inquiry, and similarly every activity and pursuit, is thought to aim at some good."

—Aristotle

An interviewer expects questions. Your questions.

How can you ask pertinent questions, if you don't know much?

Unless you demonstrate an interest in the company and the position you're hoping to fill, you're not likely to move from being the *interviewee* to being *invited in*.

Would it surprise you to learn there's a book entitled *101 Dynamite Questions to Ask at Your Job Interview*? Author Richard Fein was able to fill more than 100 pages on the subject. (Impact Publications, 1996)

Surely, you should be able to go to an interview with a few good questions at the ready.

THE DYNAMICS OF ASKING

Questions help the potential employer learn more about you.

If you're not a rocket scientist, you probably won't ask rocket science-related questions; rather, your questions will disclose more about topics that interest you. Your phrasing of questions will showcase finesse—or lack of finesse.

Do you understand what's expected of you if you assume this position? Your questions can be more revealing than answers you supply to the interviewer's questions.

Listening skills are quickly revealed when you ask a question. Do you listen carefully to the response? Do you follow up with another question or comment demonstrating you understood the response or perhaps, didn't understand? Did you listen carefully to the entire conversation up until now?

If your questions are well formed, you're probably someone whose thought process is sharp.

All these things and more you reveal to the observant interviewer when you ask questions.

WHAT DO YOU KNOW ABOUT THE COMPANY?

One survey conducted by an independent research firm reveals that not all job candidates know enough about the company in which they're seeking employment. It detracts from their position as viable job candidates.

According to an article in the November 10, 1997 issue of *Westchester County Business Journal*, "Few Job Seekers Do Their Homework When Applying for Jobs" (the name of the article).

Accountemps, a temporary staffing service, engaged an independent research firm to conduct a survey; 150 executives from 1,000 large employers were contacted and asked

> *"How frequently do job candidates demonstrate knowledge of your company or industry in interviews?"*

Their responses:	*Very infrequently*	9%
	Somewhat infrequently	29%
	Somewhat frequently	44%
	Very frequently	15%
	Don't know/no answer	3%

Why should anyone arrive at an interview without being well informed about the company and the industry?

You have nothing to gain and everything to lose.

In addition to learning about your prospective employer before the interview so you can ask relevant questions, you might discover this company isn't for you. Why accept an interview invitation if you don't want to work for the company?

If, for example, there's a management position in a plant that manufactures manual can openers, but the trend is toward the use of electric can openers, chances are you'd be climbing onto a sinking ship by accepting the job. If you discover, however, that the company is the exclusive supplier of can openers in China, where manual can openers are preferred, and has recently acquired two kitchen utensil manufacturing companies, you may be offered a job that promises a bright future.

THERE IS SUCH A THING AS A DUMB QUESTION

1. Don't ask a question if you don't know what you're talking about. The interviewer may provide an answer and then ask you something about the matter you introduced, which would put you up the proverbial creek.

> *"Does the company plan to do business abroad?"*
> *asks a plant supervisor candidate.*

> *"Our Ireland plant made international headlines last week. We installed a dynamic widgywamy to keep air clean at the plant. How do you feel about the future of widgywamies?" (Of course, you'll regain your composure.)*

> *"I've worked at plants that use Green Gus air tubing for the job. What is there about the widgywamy that makes it the cleaning apparatus of choice in Ireland?"*

2. Don't ask a tactless question.

> *"I know a Korean company purchased TQ Instruments last month. Do the American workers resent foreign ownership?"*

> *"The media finally stopped writing about the company's role in the environmental accident that killed fish at Boat's Island. How did your public relations people accomplish that?"*

> *"Is the CEO's open support of the Ibiwashi Cult's polygamous practices hurting sales?"*

True, the questions above couldn't have been formed without knowing about the companies. Still, there was nothing to be gained from having answers to these tactless questions.

That leads to the next admonition.

3. Don't ask idle questions. Idle chatter is a time waster. You'll probably tire or confuse the interviewer who wonders, why does this matter? It's not good form to waste someone's time. If you can't think of a reason the information you might receive would benefit you, don't ask the question. This rule may not apply in other settings. Your curiosity may turn up information that's important; moreover, you won't know unless you ask and time isn't always an issue. But that's not true when a job interview is in progress.

GET THE INFORMATION YOU NEED

Expand Your Reach

Things change quickly. It's not at all unusual for companies to downsize, merge, relocate, or even cease and desist. Company executives are frequently "newsmakers," and you don't want to be sitting in the interviewee's seat without knowing that the company's CEO, for example, was just awarded the Nobel Peace Prize.

Information that you picked up online or in a business magazine or newspaper a few weeks ago may already be outdated. Now more than ever you'll want up-to-the-minute information. The good news is that the Internet makes it very easy to obtain. The flip side of the good news is that not everything you read on the Internet is trustworthy. Be ready to check more than one source— and, if something sounds "off" or appears too good to be true, trust your instincts and investigate. If you can't investigate immediately, don't use the information unless or until you learn more. Access the front pages of major newspapers online to look for industry news. *The Los Angeles Times*, for example, may hint at a company merger; the *Boston Globe* may confirm there's a strong possibility; and the *Christian Science Monitor* may have something more to add on the topic.

But keep in mind: *This isn't your Grandpa's Internet.* All kinds of information sources exist and are accessible. Be creative. Try out different search engines (e.g., www.search.com) that may lead you to new sources, and don't be surprised if an old reliable search engine has changed and offers up new information. Tap into your own network of colleagues; friends, associates, sorority sisters, and so on. Use all the technology available to you, including personal cell phone and text messages. You may be able to quickly reach people who know more or who can refer you to someone who does. It's likely you'll get the feedback you seek without delay. Do you participate on social networks? Subscribers to Twitter, for example, may "reach out" to a veritable network of contacts and ask for opinions: *"Is casual dress acceptable in Boise when I interview for a marketing position"?*

If this kind of information gathering sometimes appears to be over-whelming, resist the temptation to toss in the towel! Take a deep breath and keep going. You're bound to find what you need, and frequently what you find will exceed your expectations. It's likely you'll arrive at the interview extremely well informed, and you owe it all to technology and to your willingness to make it work for you.

A Few Words About Annual Reports

◆ If a company you're interested in sells stock to the public, it will have an annual report. In the report you can learn about the company's objectives and performance, information that is especially useful to investors or potential investors. If you're short on time, you may want to quickly scan this part of the report, "inhale" some information, and go directly to the chairman's message.

◆ The chairman's message is somewhat predictable—it will review achievements, discuss challenges, and project good things for the future.

◆ You should be able to access an annual report online without incurring a fee. You may, however, have to sign in to the company's Web site in order to gain access to it. A local stockbroker's office may have the annual report you want and need. Some libraries keep annual reports in the reference section. You can always place a call to the company in question and ask to have a copy mailed to you. But, you're well advised to check the company's Web site first. If you don't have a computer and printer at your disposal, it's likely you can use one at your local library.

Marketing Material

◆ *Advertising or promotional material* is designed to impress readers. Simple questions may come to mind as you scan marketing material. It's reasonable to contact the company's sales and marketing personnel to request material. Let the person you speak with know of your intention.

> *"I want to learn all I can about your company before I'm interviewed."*

You might get more cooperation than you expected. An employee newsletter or other insider material may be sent along for your edification, too.

Industry Publications

◆ *Trade periodicals* serve as eye-openers when you want to learn more about an industry. For example, *National Jeweler* claims in its advertising to be committed to providing jewelry professionals with the most authoritative source of cutting-edge industry news available anywhere. How can you ignore this if you're interested in working in this industry? You can even subscribe to National Jeweler Network's free e-mail newsletters.

◆ Pick an industry, any industry, and you're likely to find a trade periodical that is "married" to the industry. Industry movers and shakers are spotlighted, and emerging trends don't escape notice. Advertisers feature their latest wares, and if you're intrigued and want to know more, you're likely to find 800 numbers so you can quickly call for additional information. Don't overlook the benefit of becoming familiar with industry buzzwords. Among other things, this know-how boosts self-confidence.

◆ Trade publications include: *Advertising Age, Adweek, Creative Screenwriting, Investment Adviser, Fund Strategy, Legal Week, Casino Journal*, and a long parade of other titles.

Trade publications typically engage excellent researchers and writers to produce articles. Just by reading you'll take advantage of someone else's hardcore information-gathering ability.

Television and Newspapers

You'll find it advantageous to be generally well informed; your daily newspaper and television and radio news are excellent sources of information.

◆ If you prefer, or if you're short on time, scan the Internet for news stories.

◆ Pay particular attention to business sections of a newspaper.

◆ If you don't customarily read major business periodicals, change your reading habits. Get into the habit of buying various magazines from a newsstand or subscribing to one or two favorites.

◆ Then, too, popular magazines that focus on business information can be found in most libraries and you can read one or more free of charge.

Specific information about a company and an industry are essential when you're going to be interviewed but there's no substitute for being generally well informed.

If, for example, the company has recently begun to do business in Mexico, and there's major political change in Mexico, how might this impact foreign companies doing business in Mexico? If you don't know, it's probably a good question to ask the interviewer. If you do know, you might let the interviewer know that you know.

> *"I understand the company isn't going to intro-duce the new product in Mexico, as planned. Is this due to political change?"*

(If so, and you're interviewing for a management position, can you offer a solution?)

> *"At Brundage Industries, we faced a similar chal-lenge. We waited two years before expanding our line in France. While we waited, we opened new markets in Scotland. We increased market share while minimizing risk."*

Networking with Employees

◆ *Talk* to people you know. If family members or acquaintances work for the company, ask them to tell you about the company. Don't get specific and you may pick up unexpected information.

> *"Word is the job you want is being done by an outside consultant. The company wants to hire him as an employee. If he accepts their job offer—well, you can see it wouldn't be good for you."*

◆ *Membership directories* can lead you to employees who may chat. If you both belong to the same business association, you share common ground.

> *"I found your name in the International Association of Business Communicators Membership Directory. I belong to IABC in Dallas. I have a job interview scheduled with your company's Human Resources people in New Orleans. Do you have any suggestions for me?"*

Remember, information you obtain "from the grapevine" or from people you don't know may or may not be reliable.

Or, as the articulate Benjamin Disraeli, Earl of Beaconsfield, said, "How much easier it is to be critical than to be correct."

Of course, any information, no matter the source, may or may not be reliable.

Do your homework but be ready to think on your feet.

Chapter 4

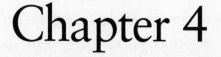

It Takes More Than New Clothes to Help You Look Good

"*So it is that the gods do not give all men gifts of grace—neither good looks nor intelligence or eloquence.*"

—Homer, c. 700 B.C.

Take a look at the umpteen resources available that spotlight business attire and grooming. Why are so many experts writing, advising, reaching out to tell others about dressing for success?

Although not everyone is good-looking, everyone can look good. And proper business attire and good grooming helps everyone project a positive image.

A professional *look* is acceptable when you keep your interview appointment. Adequate, allowable, permissible—not, you notice, dynamite!

Making a dynamite presentation takes some tweaking. You may or may not feel it's necessary to tweak. That's up to you, and many of those umpteen resources go into great detail about the kind of look you may wish to achieve for an interview and for managing your career.

Opinions about how to dress for an interview proliferate on the Internet on blogs as well as in more traditional sources. Many of the writers are well informed. You probably couldn't find one (anywhere) who wouldn't agree that first impressions make a *big* statement.

"You're going to be sized up in a hurry—in just seven seconds the interviewer will make a judgment about you—do you look right for the job?" writes JoAnna Nicholson in her book, *Dressing Smart for Men: 101 Mistakes You Can't Afford to Make . . . and How to Avoid Them* (Impact Publications, Manassas, VA, 2004; p. 128).

These are the basics for a professional look: a navy or dark suit, white shirt, conservative tie, dark shoes and socks, for men; a conservative suit, white or light-colored blouse, conservative shoes with low to mid-high heels in a color that complements the suit, as well as sheer stockings for women.

Your clothing should fit well, be clean, pressed, and in perfect repair (no loose buttons or hanging hemlines, for instance). You should be scrupulously clean with nails and hair carefully groomed. If a man's mustache or beard isn't perfectly maintained, it detracts from his appearance. Rely on a good barber to help maintain facial hair or, perhaps, opt for a professional shave. If a woman's makeup isn't applied carefully and with restraint, it detracts from her appearance. Use grooming aids that have subtle fragrances and avoid jewelry that jangles or could otherwise be distracting.

WHAT ABOUT STYLE?

As the title of this chapter suggests, "It Takes More Than New Clothes to Help You Look Good." Your *style* can set you apart from other job candidates.

A Latin proverb reminds us: "It is most true, *stilus virum arguit—* our style betrays us." Let your style reveal the best you have to offer. If that's betrayal, use it to your advantage.

Good manners are always in style

◆ Arrive a few minutes ahead of the scheduled meeting time.

◆ Be pleasant and gracious to the receptionist and everyone you meet.

◆ Stand up when you meet the interviewer and be ready to shake hands. Let the interviewer be the first to extend a hand, then offer a firm handshake.

◆ Use Mr., Ms., or Mrs. Last Name unless invited to do otherwise.

◆ Don't chew gum.

◆ Don't sit without being invited to do so.

◆ If you carry a briefcase, place it on the floor near your chair. Don't assume you can use the interviewer's desk as a staging area.

◆ Say thank you when it's time to go: "Thank you for your time." (Read about exit lines in Chapter 1.)

◆ Cell phones should be turned off and out of sight. Do this prior to entering the building! Don't resume cell phone use until you exit the premises.

Being self-assured is part of a successful interview style

◆ Make good use of body language. Sit erect. Smile. Make eye contact. Don't fidget.

◆ Speak slowly enough so that you finish each word and are easily understood.

◆ Stay focused and get to the point.

◆ Listen carefully and don't interrupt.

◆ Don't jump to conclusions. If you don't understand a question, ask for an explanation.

A positive outlook is a component of a winning style

◆ Speak well of others, or, if you can't say something nice, don't say anything at all.

◆ When the interviewer asks what was the worst/what was the best kinds of questions (such as, the most difficult boss you ever had, the most uncooperative coworker you ever knew), take care. Minimize the challenge and focus on benefits, lessons learned, solutions.

◆ When the interviewer asks questions about the future (such as, Where do you see yourself five years from now?), frame your answer in terms of achievements in the position you want now.

If you're interviewing for an assistant or entry-level position, talk about learning on the job, becoming more valuable to the company. If you're interviewing for a management position, speak of building a strong core of employees, working with colleagues to set and achieve new goals. *See yourself* enjoying the company's success and learning and growing, too, so the company continues to prosper.

A calm exterior is a style enhancer

It's possible to have a calm exterior even when you're feeling nervous. This book has information that assists you to prepare for the interview—intellectually speaking. Exercise, sleep, vitamins, good diet, drinking enough water, all contribute to one's well-being—physically speaking. Put it all together and you turn in a top performance.

HEALTHY IS AS HEALTHY DOES

To embellish and borrow a phrase from Forrest Gump's mom: Healthy is as healthy does. Your actions or inactions assist you in maintaining optimum health.

◆ *See Jill*. See Jill skip breakfast so she can catch the early train to Penn Station Newark. See Jill dash up the escalator into Gateway Center, somewhat overwhelmed by the numbers of people mulling about and the vastness of the place. See Jill accept a cup of coffee from the receptionist while she waits for the recruiter.

See Jill deflate midway into the interview. Even the adrenaline pumping from the challenge and excitement of the interview doesn't keep Jill on an even keel. She leans to the side of her chair; she works hard to concentrate.

Now, see Jill stop and consume a light breakfast and later accept a glass of water from the receptionist. See Jill maintain her good posture and powers of concentration throughout the meeting.

◆ *See Jack*. Hear Jack say "No" when Sam calls for him in the evening to go to the gym. See Jack sit in the chair and watch television. Hear Jack say "No" when Vic asks him to go for a jog in the park on Saturday morning. See Jack skip his exercise routine for two weeks. See Jack grow irritable. Notice how he isn't sending résumés to potential employers.

Now, see Jack go to the gym with Sam, jog in the park with Vic, and use some of his out-of-work time to paint the sunporch. Jack renews his job search efforts with vim and vigor.

◆ *See Barbara*. See Barbara eat large bowls of chocolate ice cream every night. See Barbara's new suit get tight around her hips. See Barbara look in the mirror before her interview and grimace at her new double chin. See the interviewer lean toward Barbara so he can hear her softly spoken responses. See the clock on the wall move forward ten minutes. See Barbara exit.

Now, see Barbara ride her exercise bicycle three nights a week. Chocolate ice cream is replaced by a bowl of fruit. Barbara rarely eats after dinner. Notice that Barbara's suit fits better. She primps in front of the mirror prior to her interview. She exudes energy when she shakes hands and she's easily heard when she speaks. See Barbara leave for her new job each morning and come home from her new job each evening.

◆ *See Ken.* Hear Ken's physician tell him to take vitamins and stop smoking. See Ken take classes in meditation. Two weeks pass. Hear a recruiter tell Ken, "It's a smoke-free work environment." Listen to Ken discuss his own success in cutting down his cigarette intake. Listen to Ken praise his physician. See the recruiter lean forward in his chair, a package of cigarettes visible in his pocket.

See Ken attend another meditation class. He brings a guest. It's someone you know. It's Ken's new coworker, the recruiter!

◆

And, so it goes.

PLUG IT IN

Taking good care of yourself especially during stressful times makes sense. These little stories may seem frivolous, but taking care of yourself is a serious, high stakes pursuit. If job offers come your way quickly, you should find relief soon. However, if the job search takes six to nine months or thereabouts, added stress becomes a long-term companion.

A stress-management book can help. Among the thousands of titles that appear when you search the Amazon Web site for books about stress is *Stress Management for Dummies*, written by Allen Elkin (and made available for reading on Kindle in July 2008). Read the book description and you'll find, "Does the hectic pace of modern life put you in a bind? Are your ulcers having ulcers? It's time to give yourself a break. *Stress Management for Dummies* can help you discover how to lower your stress level immediately." Dr. Elkin clearly makes the connection between stress and poor health.

Get the Job! Interview Strategies That Work isn't devoted to the topic of good health; it is, however, devoted to providing you with information that enables you to be successful.

Taking care of yourself isn't a sometimes thing. When you're trying to find a job, you may be inclined to drop good health habits. Don't do it. Be aware that your good health habits help you through these challenging times.

CHECK IN, CHECK UP

The following quiz is designed to red-flag behavior changes you may want to address. Consult a physician or health care professional routinely, and at any time you're concerned about a change in your regimen. Be ready to pamper yourself while you move through stressful times.

Now that I'm job hunting . . .

I've changed my *eating habits*.

Circle one:	YES	NO
I eat more sugary foods.	Y	N

	YES	NO
I eat on the run, not stopping to sit and relax when I dine.	Y	N
I've increased my alcohol intake.	Y	N
I skip meals.	Y	N
I eat at predictable times.	Y	N
I consume more fast foods.	Y	N
I eat more or less than usual.	Y	N

WHAT NOW? If you're skipping meals, eating more or less than usual, consuming sugary foods, it may contribute to sleeplessness and other unwelcome changes you attribute to job search concerns. Since good nutrition plays a major role in one's well-being, examine your habits and establish a regimen that supports your good health.

Now that I'm job hunting . . .

I've changed my *exercise* and *rest* and *relaxation* regimen.

Circle one:	YES	NO
I exercise more often.	Y	N
I watch more television.	Y	N
I'm more sedentary.	Y	N
I don't spend money on movies and other unnecessary activities.	Y	N
I have more time to jog or play ball and I take advantage of it.	Y	N

	YES	NO
Personal pleasures must take a back burner to my main pursuit: to get a job.	Y	N
I sleep more, exercise less.	Y	N
I don't sleep well. I've got my job search on my mind. I take sleeping pills.	Y	N

WHAT NOW? Persistent changes in sleep patterns and changes in exercise regimen that lead to a more sedentary lifestyle should be noted. Experts agree regular exercise is more beneficial than sporadic exercise. But no exercise is *beastly*, especially when you've had a good exercise regimen and let it lapse. Don't assume everything will fall into place once you've accepted a job offer; you've got to *want* to exercise. If you don't have an established pattern of exercise, now may be a good time to start one.

Now that I'm job hunting . . .

My *relationships* with family and friends have changed.

Circle one:	YES	NO
I'm more cautious about spending money; as a result, my leisure pursuits are canceled.	Y	N
I let friends pay my way and it bothers me.	Y	N
I spend more money on myself and others because it makes me feel better.	Y	N
I don't get many invitations anymore. I wonder if friends avoid me because I'm too serious.	Y	N

WHAT NOW? You probably need to talk with family and friends. Don't let a temporary interruption of cash flow cause you to curb activities that contribute to a fulfilling social life. Practically speaking, some expensive pursuits may have to wait. Don't just eliminate—substitute. A day on the golf course, however, may give you an opportunity to network and that supports your job search. As to money, assume your friends who reach for the check can and wish to do so. Make a mental note to return the favor when you're able. Don't dwell on what you *can't* do. Focus on what you're doing and shall accomplish.

◆

A GEM OF INFORMATION

Did you know there's something else you can do to promote the interviewer's good feelings toward you? Psychologists discovered it years ago.

People tend to act favorably toward people with whom they establish rapport. You discover and talk about things you have in common and build a relationship from that common zone.

Psychologists also discovered rapport can be established faster with a process known as *mirroring*.

Match or mirror your behavior to the interviewer's behavior—voice, breathing rhythm, body language, choice of words, and pace and pitch of speech can be so like those of the interviewer that he or she will adore you. Manipulation? Maybe. Harmful? Not unless you do it badly and make the interviewer uncomfortable.

Would you be surprised to learn that some recruiters *mirror* job candidates to make them feel at ease? "It establishes a clear and open line of communication about the job," claims one executive.

Master this strategy and you'll wield a wider sphere of influence during your next job interview. How's that for looking good! To learn more about this mind game, scan indexes in psychology textbooks and look for the words *mirroring* and *influence*.

Chapter 5

◆

Practice Makes Perfect—The Fine Art of Rehearsal

"Practice is the best of all instructors."

—Publilius Syrus, First century B.C.

WHY IS REHEARSAL IMPORTANT?

Think of each interview as a rehearsal for the next interview and you'll find it easier to think with your head and not be distracted by knees that knock or hands that quiver.

Why is each interview a rehearsal for the next interview? Because nothing takes the place of the real thing.

A pregnant woman may read everything she can read about child-birth. She may talk to women who recently delivered babies and take classes that help her master breathing exercises and teach her what to expect.

Do you think she knows more about what to expect by the time she's ready to deliver her second child? Absolutely.

You don't have to be a math whiz to remember this equation:

> *Interview = Experience*
> *Interview and Interview = More experience*
> *Experience and Experience = Ability to ace the job*
> *interview = Job offer*

Having said that, your logical starting point is preparation.

Rehearsal is an excellent preparation strategy because it helps you concentrate on what to expect and how to react.

CURTAIN UP
If you're going to rehearse, it helps to have the script.

You'll find differences in dialogue and emphasis, but your part will consistently emphasize

◆ how your skills make you a good fit for this job.

◆ how your background makes you a good fit for this job.

◆ how your experience makes you a good fit for this job.

While you're doing this, you'll strive to

◆ show good judgment about the topics you introduce.

- use positive language.

- give focused answers.

- demonstrate you're verbally fluent (such as using proper grammar and a well-rounded vocabulary).

- display self-confidence and especially a *sense of self*; know what you want now and indicate you've considered future goals.

THREE DIFFERENT SCRIPTS

Human Resources professionals talk about several kinds of employment interviews:

1. **Behavioral** The interviewer puts the focus on personal conduct, your *modus operandi*.

   Illustration:

   > *Tell me about the last time you had a conflict with a coworker. What happened? When a coworker complains or gossips about the boss, how do you respond? If you don't get approval for taking a day off, and you really need the time, what will you do about it?*

2. **Situational** The interviewer targets challenges and specific choices you might have to make.

   Illustration:

   > *If you realized you couldn't meet a deadline, would you get help or, take work home? If an associate gave a client the wrong information,*

would you correct that associate in front of the client, in private, or not at all? If you promise to telephone an important customer but it's quitting time and you still don't have the necessary information, will you call before you leave the office or wait until tomorrow when you have the required data?

3. **Tell me about yourself** The interviewer searches for how you see yourself and whether you're direct or tend to be a fence-sitter.

Illustration:

Why should we hire you? What are your strong points? Are you willing to travel? Do you prefer to work alone? Are you good at prioritizing? How do you feel about attending meetings?

4. **Other** You may discover other scripts when you interview and you may meet interviewers who don't follow any script, but if you rehearse using portions of the three scripts listed above, you'll be well prepared when the curtain goes up. No matter which script is in use, your responses should be the good fit responses mentioned earlier.

How your skills make you a good fit for this job
How your background makes you a good fit for this job
How your experience makes you a good fit for this job

THE REST OF THE CAST

Even if you're putting on a one-person performance, you need a supporting crew.

Enlist the help of a roommate, spouse, significant other, friend—anyone who is supportive—not simply agreeable but interested in your success and ready to call it like he or she sees it. If your supporting crew member is inclined to be overly critical, you may find yourself thinking, With a friend like this, who needs enemies? On the other hand, you need constructive criticism if you're to fine-tune your performance.

If your support person is agreeable, work with an Evaluation Checklist. Use the components listed above and devise a Rating System (Good, Needs Improvement, and so on).

For example:

> *Uses Positive Language:*
> *Good [ ]   Needs Improvement [ ]   Poor [ ]*
>
> *Gives Focused Answers:*
> *Good [ ]   Needs Improvement [ ]   Poor [ ]*

TELL ME MORE

You'll also want to know about:

◆ **Voice**—Are you easily heard? Do you use a good pace and pitch?

◆ **Eye contact**

◆ **Smile**

◆ **Body language**

and anything you think of as a needs-improvement point. If, for example, you fidget when you're nervous, ask to be rated on your composure.

Use your completed Checklist as a guide to sharpen performance. If you wish, use the same list again, adding additional rating columns, to indicate whether you've improved.

You may not put on a dress rehearsal but you may want to get an opinion about your interview outfit.

Second opinions can be valuable. Ask as much or as little of your trusty *stagehand* as meets your needs.

PLUG IT IN!

Tape your session so you can listen to it later. Use a video camera if you think it will benefit your evaluation and help you improve your performance. Work in front of a mirror if you won't be distracted by your reflection. (It's amazing to see how one's posture improves after a glance in the mirror reveals—dare it be mentioned?—slouching.)

The staging area can be well appointed if that makes the rehearsal more meaningful. Let the "interviewer" sit behind a desk if you need to reinforce your skills at making eye contact, using appropriate vocal pitch, or making a graceful exit; but don't skip a rehearsal because you don't have time to set up a staging area. A rehearsal without benefit of props is perfectly acceptable.

If you work with an executive search firm, outplacement consultants, or professionals who are assisting you to get a job, you may have a built-in crew at your disposal.

TWO-WAY DIALOGUE

Invite the stand-in to ad-lib and listen carefully to what's said. In addition to asking the questions you provide on script, improvisation will keep you both alert and the performance will be more valuable. Explain to our support person that questions may be behavioral, situational, or "tell me about yourself" queries. Begin by using questions discussed in this chapter; later, the stand-in should find it easy to perform extemporaneously.

Listening is a valuable skill that helps boost sales success. You're selling yourself at the interview and you'll want to make sure you understand the end result benefits or *herbs* the buyer seeks.

Herbs spice up a dish and when you offer <u>E</u>nd <u>R</u>esult <u>B</u>enefits to the interviewer, you spice up your sales pitch. It becomes far more appealing. If the key word *herb* helps you remember the goal, use it! Your insight will help you get specific about

◆ how your skills make you a good fit for this job.

◆ how your background makes you a good fit for this job.

◆ how your experience makes you a good fit for this job.

No matter how much you've learned about the company and the job beforehand, you typically learn more about specific job requirements during the interview. One way you'll do this is by asking questions, too.

Another component of the rehearsal process is to recognize cues. When the interviewer talks about the company and the job, it's a good time to ask questions. Read more about this in Chapter 3.

Sometimes, the interviewer will ask, "Do you have any questions?"

Ask a question. Ask two questions.

If you listen carefully, you'll be able to ask a sensible question or two with ease. To do less would suggest you're not interested in the company or the job.

Use rehearsals to help you grow accustomed to asking questions.

POSITIONING

The 1997 book, *Get What You Deserve* (Avon Books) spotlights Powerful Personal Marketing Techniques. Authors Jay Levinson and Seth Godin also wrote *Guerrilla Marketing* (Houghton Mifflin, 1998), reportedly one of the best-selling marketing series of all time.

Levinson and Godin discuss a concept known as *positioning*—making something fit into a category—appealing, indisputable, and memorable. Best-selling products are positioned.

Ben & Jerry's ice cream, for example, is made by down-to-earth people who care about the important things in life. Does this describe ice cream?

No, but it does describe Ben & Jerry's.

Appealing, indisputable, memorable.

Seven-Up is the Uncola. Anything that people find objectionable about cola drinks—well, Seven-Up is the opposite. Seven-Up didn't change its taste, but when it became the Uncola, sales zoomed!

What does this have to do with the fine art of rehearsal?

Since it's impossible for you to work with an exact script, you'll position yourself every time you speak about

◆ how your skills make you a good fit for this job.

◆ how your background makes you a good fit for this job.

◆ how your experience makes you a good fit for this job.

You'll deliver winning dialogue—appealing, indisputable, and memorable—when you position yourself well.

Use rehearsal as a time to practice advertising your position. Examine the impact of the words you choose. And, if you haven't consciously assessed your "position" before, do it now.

Chapter 6

What You Should
Know About the
Personalities That
Interviewers Adopt

"It is most true—stilus virum arguit—our style betrays us."

—A Latin Proverb

GOOD COP/BAD COP

Most people know about the good cop/bad cop routine. The so-called good cop earns favor with the person being interrogated. The individual is more likely to confess to the good cop. Interviewers adopt work-time personalities, too. It helps them do their jobs.

The good cop/bad cop technique may be old but it still works. If you find yourself assessing whether or not you like these company representatives . . . ask yourself if one of them is playing "bad cop." It's tough to be manipulated by this technique, or any other, when you identify it as a setup.

Interviewers who want to assess how well candidates behave under pressure may find the good cop/bad cop personality a tempting choice.

The good guy/bad guy routine, for example, may soften the job candidate so he or she will agree to share an assistant when the work load suggests that a full-time assistant is justified. Or, if you find yourself aligned with the good guy, you may offer concessions without being asked to because you feel that you should support the good guy.

STAGES OF PROGRESS

1. *Greetings:* An interviewer may be constrained when greeting you. The surroundings can be pleasant and comfortable but you're not encouraged to make yourself comfortable.

   Are you getting the message this isn't going to be easy?

   or

   An interviewer acts as though he or she has known you for ages: "Make yourself comfortable. Would you prefer coffee or a cold drink? I understand you're to be congratulated on earning your degree. What are your plans for graduate school?"

   Are you getting the message this is friendly and focused on "wonderful you"?

2. *Moving right along:* That constrained individual comes around from behind the desk and takes a seat near you. He discusses his son's plans to attend law school.

   Are you surprised by the sudden intimacy?

   or

You find yourself talking about your trip to Paris and you can't recall the question you were asked.

Does it occur to you that you've forgotten why you're here?

3. *Winding-up:* "We're interviewing several job candidates. Check with Ms. Meyers at the desk before you leave. Thank you for coming." Mr. Constrained/Intimate is out the door before you can pick up your briefcase.

Does that earlier feeling of discomfort set in?

or

You're asked if you know how to get back to the highway? "Let me walk you to the elevator," insists this interviewer who is focused on wonderful you. You, however, haven't a clue about what just transpired. A job offer? Anyone's guess is as good as yours.

YOUR MODUS OPERANDI

Logic suggests personalities, moods, identities that interviewers display vary. So, what should you know about them?

> *The most proficient interviewers you encounter are not making accidental comments or moving in uncharted waters.*

> *What is it you should know about yourself?*

> *You don't have to make accidental comments or move in uncharted waters.*

Know what you want to accomplish. Take every opportunity to do so. Once you plan to act and not just react, the interviewer's personality or identity won't matter to you. You'll find your way within the context of the environment provided to accomplish your goals.

"The controlling intelligence understands its own nature, and what it does, and whereon it works," is a comment attributed to Marcus Aurelius Antoninus more than 1,000 years ago. The wisdom of the observation is as valid today as it was then.

Take charge and get what you want!

Chapter 7

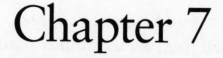

What Professional Interviewers Look for in a Job Candidate

*"Ask, and it shall be given you; seek,
and ye shall find; knock, and it shall be
opened unto you."*

—Luke 11:9

While you're scrambling to make a good impression and get a job offer, the interviewer is trying to find the best person for the job—the one who will receive the job offer. The more you know about the interviewer's quest, the better prepared you can be to deliver the goods.

In a large company, you'll probably talk with a recruiter and then a department manager. In a smaller company, the "boss" may conduct the interview.

"Recruiting is a filtration process," observes one recruiter. When he recruits on a college campus, he typically starts with hundreds of job candidates and quickly whittles that number down to dozens. He looks for people who fit his company's corporate culture.

FITTING-IN IS A RECURRING THEME

In *Conducting Better Job Interviews* (Barron's Business Success Series, 1991), author Robert F. Wilson writes: "All recruiting and hiring decisions should be based on a single question: Is this decision consistent with our corporate mission?"

Two professional Human Resources interviewers were interviewed about interview strategies. The Q & A sessions are transcribed here. Some of the questions and comments have been paraphrased so the information is presented without digression—an easy thing to do when both the professional Human Resources person and the interviewer are enthusiastic about the topic and eager to talk.

A LITTLE BACKGROUND INFORMATION

Lizandra Vega has been an Executive Recruiter for fifteen years and is a Founding Partner of Perennial Resources International (www.perennialresources.com), a full-service search firm located in New York City. She is a Certified Image Consultant and her book *The Image of Success: Make a Great Impression and Land the Job You Want* is slated to be published by AMACOM Books in the spring of 2010.

Question/comment: What's your background as it relates to knowing what interviewers look for in a job candidate?

Response: I've been in recruiting for fifteen years. The last six years have been with Perennial Resources.

[Ms. Vega recently took some time away from interviewing to write her book.]

Question/comment: Would it be fair to say that you interview or prepare candidates for interviews?

Response: Yes.

Question/comment: What would you say are the critical considerations for someone who is interviewing, no matter what position they wish to fill?

Response: Making sure the person is a "fit" for the job in terms of criteria, experience, and educational background. Many times candidates feel that recruiters are not thinking outside the box. *Why am I not being seen for this position?* They don't realize how many people are being considered for *this position.* It's very important for the recruiter to f-o-c-u-s on job specifics. I would add that the presentation of the résumé is important. It's the first *hint* you get.

Question/comment: Would it be important for people to have different résumés available?

Response: Yes. Absolutely. One résumé doesn't represent the many facets of one person, and when you're trying to open your market—when you add too many things to one résumé, it looks like you're all over the place. I wouldn't say prepare ten résumés but let's say three résumés that focus on three of the top areas you want to pursue. Let's say I have a recruiting background but I also have an image-consulting background. So I would write a résumé that's purely *recruiting* and a résumé that is purely *image consulting* and then a general résumé. I would submit the résumé that best "fits" the job.

Question/comment: Is it important for the Objective portion of the résumé to be very specific?

Response: I'm not a fan of the Objective Statement. I know it's classic, but it could cause difficulty if it's not worded a certain way. I'm not saying I'm anti–Objective Statement. I think that people often make them very wordy. Sometimes when the candidate doesn't have enough experience, he or she will use it to fill space.

Question/comment: Should a job candidate put in the necessary effort to perfect the Objective Statement?

Response: Some people write a Summary and not an Objective. A Summary acts like a commercial about who you are, and it can be done in bullet-point format.

Question/comment: Would you place the Summary at the top of the résumé?

Response: Yes. You could call it a Qualification Summary.

Question/comment: When you're hiring are you thinking about the person's potential with the firm?

Response: It depends on the job level that must be filled. If you're hiring for a mid-level or senior position you will consider where that person might be in three years, but if you're hiring a receptionist or administrative person you may not want that person to have high expectations. You want the person to stay with the job.

Comment: Another expert told me it's extremely important for the job candidate to focus on the job they wish to have and nothing more.

Response: My take on it is you always want to keep yourself open for learning, training within the company, within your position. But for the interview, it's extremely important to focus on the position at hand.

Question/comment: You've been doing this work for fifteen years; what changes in the process are most outstanding?

Response: The communication network is much more sophisticated. You have to present yourself through different mediums that were not available ten or fifteen years ago. These days if someone asks me if they can "fax" a résumé, I think, *Really? Is this a person who is afraid of technology?* The candidates have to be versatile. You never know which medium the recruiter will prefer. There are recruiters who prefer to chat or communicate through e-mail or on a BlackBerry. Some will pick up the phone and want to hear a voice. I spoke to one person in Atlanta who could see me via her iChat. *[iChat is an instant-messaging application using text and video.]*

Question/comment: Shouldn't job candidates be thinking about what they can offer to the company?

Response: Absolutely. The candidate wants to let it be known, *I'm here to make things easier for the company*. He or she is selling and doesn't want to sound like it's all about *me, me, me*.

Question/comment: Do interviewers still ask candidates, "Where do you see yourself in five years?"

Response: Yes. People ask it a lot because they want to see how quickly you envision yourself moving up the ranks. In some cases it's good to appear ambitious. In some cases, this is detrimental. So what I suggest is stay on the safe side. "I see myself within the company, or within my next home . . . hopefully with additional responsibilities and an opportunity for learning." Don't use the word "growth"—it's a killer. "Growth" seems like you want a prestigious title, more money.

Question/comment: It's *me-me-me* again.

Response: Yes. A little too demanding. The candidate can "throw it back" to the recruiter: "Whatever the company thinks I can handle." It's always about what you can do for them.

Question/comment: If a recruiter is looking for someone who can work independently and off-site, what demonstrates that the person can be productive in that setting?

Response: If you're referring to employees who won't have high visibility—who might work in a back-office, for example—I would be more lenient about personal appearance, but the candidate's communication skills would have to be superb. The person would have to demonstrate great diction, articulation, and sound "nice" on the telephone. Sounding "nice" is important. The candidate shouldn't be easily flustered by too many questions. Customer-service people have to be patient and be problem solvers, too.

Question/comment: How do you elicit this information from them?

Response: I would use a "situational" type of interview. I would ask the individual to give me an example of a scenario I think she would encounter in her position. I don't want to trick anyone. If the candidate worked in a high-volume call center, I might ask, "What are the steps you take to prioritize? What have you done in the past that helped you handle these types of hectic situations?"

Question/comment: When you're interviewing, do you adopt different personas? Do you sometimes appear more stern, or do you soften your tone? Are you aware of making personal changes in how you present yourself to different candidates?

Response: I'm pretty much myself all the time. I will adjust according to what I'm getting back from the person. If I have a person who looks very nervous, I will try to put the person at ease. I never sit directly across from the individual. It seems too confrontational. I'll sit on the side. And I'll tilt my chair in a more engaging position. My style is very engaging, very conversational. I think a stiff, "I'm in charge" approach is a little antiquated these days. Of course, if a candidate were to be disrespectful I would change my demeanor.

I want to be the job candidate's partner in getting the job. I am the leader because I invited the person in to interview with me. But, my style is not to intimidate. My style is to make candidates comfortable enough so they're happy to talk with me, share with me. I'm quick to smile. A smile can do wonders to relax a person and keep a conversation moving forward.

Question/comment: Can you introduce personal information?

Response: It's very tricky to talk about personal information, because there are some things you're not supposed to ask. I might give an anecdote that has to do with the office. I could say

something like, "One time when I hired a person. . . ." If I offer a personal anecdote it would relate to business.

Question/comment: Is there o-n-e thing you would like to tell anybody about getting a job offer?

Response: Ask for the job! So many times people seem like they're interested; their body language suggests they are interested, and the recruiter says to herself, *Well, they seem interested, but I don't know.* If you ask for the job, that means you're going to accept it. There's not going to be a song and dance about counteroffers and this and that. If I were choosing between two candidates and felt torn between the two of them, if one asked for the job that would be the thing that would get me to make the decision. *You know what? This person asked for the job!*

Further, I always like it when we're closing the interview, and the candidate is about to thank me for my time and shake hands, and the candidate says, "I would really like this job." *Be bold about it!*

◆

A LITTLE BACKGROUND INFORMATION

Kathy Klein is Vice President, Career Blazers, a division of Global Employment Solutions, Inc. Career Blazers is a full-service, professional staffing firm charged with finding and hiring people to fill temporary and direct-hire positions for their clients. Ms. Klein works in the New York City office.

───────────◆───────────

Question/comment: How long have you been doing interview work?

Response: I've been at Career Blazers for about twenty-three years and doing the interviewing for our staff for the last twenty-one years.

Question/comment: What kind of staff is hired?

Response: I hire sales staff for my division.

Question/comment: Are there frequent staff changes?

Response: I have a commitment to hiring entry-level salespeople but that does cost me enormous turnover in the beginning because most people who have never sold before don't have any perception about what the real activity is like.

Question/comment: What are you looking for?

Response: Entry-level salespeople are not necessarily entry-level to the workforce. When I came to Career Blazers I was an entry-level salesperson but I had nine years of prior work experience and nine years of full-time motherhood. So, entry-level is simply entry-level to this business or to sales, in general. I hire recent college graduates on occasion, but more often people transitioning from something else. What you must look for is a quality that's almost impossible to measure and that's motivation. People who are outside of sales do not understand the extraordinary amount of drive you need to get started in a sales career.

Question/comment: Is there some way to make this clear to a job candidate?

Response: I'm unfailingly candid about just how frustrating it is but when people are job seekers they tend to not really listen to the bad part. They focus on securing a position, and a safe harbor sounds better than no harbor. Many people think of a career in sales because people tell them they have the personality for it. I try to assure people that sales has little to do with personality. Personality might make you Queen of the Prom but not make you an excellent salesperson. Sales is truly about an extraordinary amount of drive and commitment because we do an extraordinary amount of phone work, cold-calling. Cold-calling is not like chatting on the phone and cold-calling can be extremely futile and frustrating, unless you're truly driven by the financial rewards of sales, or you're a goal-driven person who needs to produce because you need to be the best and you do it for the glory. In the absence of one of those motivations you're doomed for failure.

Question/comment: How can you judge whether someone can handle rejection?

Response: It's impossible to judge, in my opinion, and I've been doing it for ten years.

Question/comment: You just raised another point—professional interviewers realize there are certain areas where they will be bumping up against a wall.

Response: I feel that way. I don't know if all of our clients share that view because most of our clients are interviewers, too. I don't put extraordinary faith in my judgment. I think I've been right many times and wrong many times.

Question/comment: So, a professional interviewer stands in the middle between the job candidate and somebody else.

Response: Precisely. When I prepare people to go out there for interviews, I use this analogy: The interviewer, who is typically the first-line person you meet, is like a goalie in hockey, an obstacle between you and the job. Impress the interviewer so you can overcome whatever is set in front of you and don't let the interviewer deny you the right to get closer to that job and see what it's all about.

Question/comment: That's a very vivid word picture. Do you think it frightens some people?

Response: Maybe. I also tell them how to get past that person. You need to present yourself in a particular light. You need to parry difficult questions. I've done a lot of coaching for interview preparation. I've listened to interviewees. I'm not as easy to get past as some.

Question/comment: What does the professional interviewer look for in a job candidate?

Response: It's going to vary depending on whether it's an entry-level candidate or someone with significant prior work experience. When someone has significant prior work experience, it's going to take a stable work history. All interviewers would like to believe that someone they are going to hire would like to remain in the company, although not necessarily in that position, for a significant period of time. In the current workplace, peoples' histories tend to be less stable than they were years ago. People rarely stay in companies 10, 15, or 25 years as they formerly did. Stability, however, can be viewed as a great virtue. It certainly speaks to never having interpersonal conflicts because people who tend to be contentious don't stay in one place very long. Stability implies being conscientious because you're not kept in a company very long if you're not. So, it really sums up so many attributes in an employee if they remain in one place for a long period of time.

Question/comment: Let's say that someone is not able to show a stable work history for a lot of good reasons.

Response: That person better be very good at articulating those reasons.

Question/comment: In this very mobile society, a spouse may have to move to take advantage of an excellent job opportunity.

Response: Precisely. Then the spouse must move too.

Question/comment: I also envision companies that close or downsize and very capable people are dismissed through no faults of their own. So, is it important to articulate these things?

Response: Yes. One must go into an interview well prepared, armed with good solid reasons. If, for example—and this is frequently the case—in an aging society such as ours, people are taking care of a sick relative, they've got to go into the interview being able to express that they're now able to make a 100 percent commitment. You can't leave an interviewer hanging, and I can't ask the candidate if that relative has met his or her end. It's not an appropriate thing for me to ask, but, I would appreciate it if someone would volunteer that information.

Question/comment: That's an interesting point. Interviewers are also bound by legal restrictions. Is it a good idea for the interviewee to be aware of what can't be asked and therefore be ready to volunteer certain information?

Response: Well, if someone was on maternity leave, for example, and is returning to the workforce, she should be very up-front about the childcare situation so an interviewer won't be concerned.

Question/comment: So, we can view the interviewer as someone who has normal concerns about reasonable things like stability. Is there something else that's outstanding?

Response: Commitment to the job at hand. A job can be a springboard to something else but interviewers don't want to see it that way. There's an open job to be filled and it's never a good idea for someone to express that they'll put up with that job as long as there's a promise of more down the road.

Question/comment: In that case, how would you suggest that somebody handle the question, "Where do you see yourself in five years?"

Response: I would love to make a home in this company.

Question/comment: Okay.

Response: Very vague.

Question/comment: So, there are times for specific answers and times for very vague answers.

Response: Vague answers generally are the best unless you're being asked about your work history.

Question/comment: How does the interviewer assess very vague answers?

Response: Well, it depends. For questions such as "Where do you see yourself in five years?" the vague answer is the appropriate answer. I interviewed someone not long ago and was able to get her to admit that what she really wanted to be was a documentary filmmaker. Because I do not hire future documentary filmmakers, she talked herself out of a job.

Question/comment: That must be a delicate balance for a candidate to maintain—being yourself, being relaxed enough so that you can be conversational, and at the same time not saying things that come to mind when you are relaxed, things that can quickly boot you out the door.

Response: When I prepare people for interviews, I tell them to consider the first interview, not when they're meeting the group they're going to work with, but when they're interviewing with the HR person, as an exclusionary process. Make sure they're not one of the nine people who is going to be excluded.

Question/comment: So, you have to be very alert throughout.

Response: Precisely. It's like walking though a minefield of conversation. You never know where a question is really going. I'll always compliment a recent college grad—because I do interview so many of them—on academic credentials and I will segue into what the person's grad school plans are. Now, here, I'm hiring people for long-term careers. I have no interest in someone with grad school aspirations. They don't understand that when I'm complimenting their credentials.

Question/comment: Are interviewers generally doing things like that?

Response: I think so. It's the only way they can ferret out those they want to hire. You need to use those strategies as an interviewer.

Question/comment: How do candidates conduct themselves without being so nervous they can't open their mouths when they get there?

Response: They need to be charming and relaxed. They need to listen to the questions and only answer what they've been asked, to be very specific when questioned about their background, education, work history. They must be very vague when questioned about the future. When most people change jobs, do they really know where they're going to be in five years?

Question/comment: I think it's a strange question to ask but, I understand it is asked.

Response: It's asked regularly. I never ask it.

Question/comment: Are there things candidates can judge about the personality of the person who is going to interview them? For example, what if they see an orderly desk as opposed to a chaotic desk?

Response: I'm glad you're not here! [*This was a telephone interview. Laughter.*]

Question/comment: A chaotic desk can speak to something that's not necessarily negative. Is there anything to be learned from that?

Response: That's a scary place to go. Today, companies have virtual offices where the person sitting there to interview you may not have personal effects. I know people are nervous but I'm a little annoyed when people walk in and feel compelled to comment about the view from my window.

Question/comment: That's interesting.

Response: I'm thinking, "Let's do what we're here for."

Question/comment: Not so long ago, I was being interviewed and I was awed by the executive's spectacular view.

Response: Well, mine is not spectacular. It's quite ordinary. It looks out over the street but it's only five floors up. We're not seeing anything remarkable.

Question/comment: Well, this woman's office was *hanging out* on the top of Newark, New Jersey. But, that's another important point—should the job seeker be cautious about small talk?

Response: Definitely. You never know what the personal issues are of the person you're interviewing with and if you comment about art on the walls, it may not have been that person's choice and some people think it's inappropriate. It's better to not make small talk than to make the wrong small talk.

Question/comment: What else are you looking for in a job candidate?

Response: I'm concerned somewhat about appearance. I think that if someone doesn't have the judgment to know to wear a suit to an interview, I'm concerned about that person's judgment in general. I don't care about the style of the suit. I'm not talking about appearance in that respect. But the way you dress for an interview speaks about your judgment. If I'm interviewing a young man and he has not recently shaved or doesn't have decently shined shoes, it shows he didn't understand what was appropriate for an interview. If a woman comes in with three-inch-long acrylic nails with designs on them, I would have an issue with it.

Question/comment: What if an interviewer is seeking a job candidate for work in the mailroom?

Response: A person who is in a back-office position should be judged solely based on background and commitment.

Question/comment: What if someone for that position comes in looking like he or she is ready to be the Chief Executive Officer, does that confuse the interviewer? Should you look the part?

Response: Well, I don't think you can look too good for an interview although one doesn't come dressed in a tuxedo for an interview. But, I'm sort of a Doubting Thomas. If someone came in with credentials that were overly qualified for the job at hand, I'd be very curious about any gaps in the background and be very concerned about where and why this person has been forced to take so many steps back.

Question/comment: Why might a person come in who is over-qualified?

Response: If someone was licensed in the financial markets, for example, and was found guilty of misconduct and perhaps had been incarcerated and lost the license, I would be very concerned if that person were applying for a position in the mailroom.

Question/comment: Supposedly an interviewer is not to hold certain things against job candidates.

Response: I'm not going to get into the legalities of this because it's not something I come up against. Felony convictions are public record.

Question/comment: We've talked about commitment to the job at hand. What happens if the interviewer is asking such a stream of questions the candidates feel they don't have an opportunity to make their case?

Response: Well, if the interviewer is still asking questions, there should be time for the candidate to do so.

Question/comment: Speaking of time, what about arriving on time for the interview?

Response: You should always be on time. I think it shows bad judgment to walk in 20 minutes, 30, or 40 minutes early. If I'm scheduled to meet with someone at 10:00 I don't want to be put on edge at 20 minutes before 10:00 when they show up in my reception area. I feel pressured to get out there and I really get upset by it. Perhaps not everybody does, but because I hire people who are going to go out and call on clients, I'm really concerned about their judgment.

Question/comment: So you're looking at anything that is a tip-off. In other words, you learn something about the person when your assistant comes in to announce that the candidate has arrived.

Response: I tell people who are preparing, even my daughter, when she was preparing for her first really serious job, to allow themselves an extraordinary amount of time to get to the interview because they never want to be late to an interview—that's inexcusable. But, by the same token, never show up more than five minutes early.

Question/comment: So it's not sufficient to announce to the receptionist that you're too early, you have a ten o'clock appointment, and you're going to take a seat.

Response: You know, there are certain things I'm easy about and certain things I'm tough about. Because I hire people who are going out to visit clients, to me that's a no-compromise.

Question/comment: So what may not be important to one interviewer may be a pet peeve of another?

Response: It depends on what the job is. If someone is being hired to be a receptionist, one of the preeminent responsibilities is being on time in the morning; therefore, being ten minutes late for a receptionist job interview is unforgivable. You don't get the job. On the other hand, if someone is looking for a Ph.D. in biophysics and that person will work alone in a laboratory through the middle of the night, and work in independent projects, time wouldn't be an issue and arriving ten minutes late would be of no consequence.

Question/comment: Except as a courtesy to the interviewer.

Response: Different slack is cut for different people at different job levels.

Question/comment: Your example really gets to the heart of it. Moving along—what about a person who comes into the interview with a briefcase full of material to show to you, perhaps writing samples, is there anything special you're watching for?

Response: That's something I don't come into contact with but, in general, things should never be volunteered if they're not asked for.

Question/comment: I suspect you're not too happy if someone leans in and takes over your desk.

Response: Once someone took my nameplate off my desk and was playing with it. I was mesmerized, wondering if he had any idea about what he was doing.

Question/comment: Do you think it was because of nervousness?

Response: Utter nervousness. It was humorous. I just watched this person tossing my nameplate from hand to hand. He couldn't possibly have known what he was doing.

Question/comment: I suppose interviewers have seen it all and some of it will be excused, but the person going to the interview shouldn't view it that way.

Response: Right. You would certainly excuse more in someone who is new to the workplace than you would if someone had more work history and had been through it many times. You're supposed to learn wisdom over time and if you've been on interviews 30 times in your life, you should be better at it than if it's your third interview since coming out of college.

(Many thanks to Ms. Lizandra Vega and Ms. Kathy Klein for their time and candor.)

Chapter 8

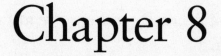

Interviews That Come in Multiples (First Interview, Second Interview)

"I think the necessity of being ready increases. Look to it."

—Abraham Lincoln

The interview concludes with an invitation to return. After you applaud yourself for being invited back, you'll want to be ready to fine-tune your strategy.

Know beforehand the six questions considered permissible to ask, which enable you to put the right focus on the next meeting.

1. Whom will I be meeting?

2. Is the interviewer someone I'd work with directly?

3. Is there anything I should bring along to show to Mr. X (such as writing samples)?

4. Now that you and I have spent time together, is there something we discussed that you think I should be sure to mention to Mr. X?

5. Could you give me an employee newsletter or other reading material that would help me prepare for the meeting?

6. Does Mr. X report to the Vice President of Marketing or the CEO? (Your knowledge of the company's organizational chart— who reports to whom—gives you a better idea of what to expect (such as who has decision-making power).

These six questions above pass the test.

The first interviewer puts you in a favorable light or you wouldn't be "held over." You'd be ignoring a great opportunity if you didn't ask questions. Of course, you'll ask the obvious—where and when?

When you ask questions of an interviewer, keep the following rules in mind:

1. Be candid and honest.

2. Speak with authority.

3. Refrain from small talk.

4. Don't introduce "*I can't do topics . . .*"—without a compelling reason (e.g., the job is in Australia, and you're not willing to move to Australia.)

5. If you're not sure *this person* has authority to answer your questions; don't ask them.

Some of these tips can be used when you get into the more delicate subject of discussing salary expectations.

SHOW ME THE MONEY

◆ Don't discuss salary with the wrong person! It's a waste of time; moreover, this indiscretion can leave you feeling foolish.

◆ If the answer is obvious, don't ask. If the job salary has been advertised, the interviewer has a right to assume you're satisfied or you wouldn't be there. Nevertheless, if you subscribe to the notion that everything is negotiable, you may want to ask if the starting salary is negotiable. If you have something special to offer—such as a facility with a second language—which will impact your effectiveness in the position, you have good reason to pursue the subject. Wage and salary guidelines are carefully established in some companies and the job you're hired for has a job level designation and a salary designation. Management bound by guidelines has nothing to discuss.

◆ Know what you're talking about; for example, if you state that the current job description matches the job description you have or had in another company where wages are higher, you should be able to back up what you say; otherwise, you offer a no-win argument and, what is more important, your trustworthiness is suspect.

THE MORE YOU KNOW

You may have one interview immediately following another, or you may be invited back at a later date. In either case, when you ask questions, listen carefully to responses.

If you have time, jot down the answers so you won't forget details. If you move from one interview to the next, without pause, you'll remember the salient points if you focused on the responses.

There's not much point in asking questions or gathering information if you don't use it to your best advantage.

Scenario

Heather Sams met the company recruiter and immediately afterward was introduced to the Director of Company Policy. Heather was interviewing for a position as a Policy and Procedure Specialist and knew the director would be her boss if she was hired. Heather mentioned two challenges in a manufacturing environment that carefully written company policy addressed. The director told Heather how she tackled those problems in a similar fashion. There was an air of friendliness throughout the interview and Heather was able to assure the director she was free to travel and handle many of the tasks the job required. She left feeling that she would get a job offer as not too many people had the experience she could bring to the job. She was called back for a third interview with the director's boss. She thought of this interview as a formality and believed the director wanted to hire her. She chatted amiably, repeating some of what she told the director, and tried to showcase her enthusiasm and desire to work for this company. The conversation wandered from topic to topic. Heather talked about operating her own business as an independent writer and was enthusiastic about her accomplishments. The vice president dismissed her after one hour and mentioned they were interviewing several candidates and it would take a few weeks before a decision was made. Heather was disappointed. When she evaluated this meeting, she realized she had talked too much. At the least, she drew attention to the fact that she had no experience working in a large corporation. She didn't get a job offer.

Issue

Don't treat any introduction or interview as a *formality*. Don't compromise the winning job strategies you master—ever. If Heather knew more about the last interviewer, especially the answers to questions 1–6 (pages 84–85), she could have been prepared to sell him on her ability to do the job. She might have recognized he was a company man and not predisposed to someone who didn't have work experience within the corporate culture.

MONEY MATTERS

You may be asked how much money you need. Or a variation of that question. You can

◆ give an acceptable range, such as $40,000 to $49,000.

◆ answer with a question. What does management have in mind?

◆ mention a figure that was advertised: I was told this job will pay $59,000 to $70,000 depending on experience.

◆ move the conversation in another direction.

The subject of money is a delicate one. Consider the following:

1. You're in a better position to discuss money *after* the potential employer is convinced the company must have you. This enviable position generally comes later in your employment career.

2. If no amount of money is mentioned and hasn't been discussed prior to interview time, you and management may be miles apart in your assessment of what the job is worth. You may be wasting valuable time if you don't offer or inquire about a salary range.

3. Money or remuneration comes under other headings, too. Annual salary that's offset by comprehensive health insurance, tuition reimbursement, and/or other valuable perquisites can be significant. You may be able to bargain for additional fringe benefits if you learn the annual salary is less than you expected. Be creative. Could you earn additional income as an instructor in a local junior college if you had time? More time off may be something the prospective employee will concede.

4. If you give the impression you're dissatisfied, the offer may not be forthcoming. If you're hired, your salary may be increased to a more agreeable level after your first performance review. Many experts who believe everything is negotiable also say timing is a key factor. Don't rely on the first part of that equation without factoring in the importance of timing. This can be a successful technique when coupled with maintaining a list of tasks you perform and comparing it to the company's printed job description. You may demonstrate you do more than you were initially hired to do. A new, accurate job description may warrant a salary increase. You'll need a printed job description for comparison purposes and you may find no evidence to support this argument.

In the final analysis, you're negotiating. Negotiating, bargaining, engineering, masterminding, settling—all similar concepts and all essential whether you like it or not. Of course, there are some salaries that are announced and no one expects them to be negotiated. Take it or leave it is the rationale.

What is the industry standard salary for this work? How much does the geographic region contribute to tinkering with the industry standard? How much competition do you have? Mr. Lincoln's words at the beginning of this chapter. "I think the necessity of being ready increases," apply.

You're well served by knowing the answers to these questions before you arrive for a first interview but the necessity of being ready increases in subsequent interviews because all parties approach the final decision stage.

You're well served by reading more about the dynamics of negotiation.

Chapter 9

◆

When Some Interview Questions Are Asked That Are Not Allowed

"*Tis with our judgments as our watches, none go just alike, yet each believes his own.*"

—Alexander Pope

The interviewer isn't permitted to ask you questions about your race, color, or religion, or who to notify in case of an emergency. (This last question can't be asked if you're not an employee!)

While interviewers are not allowed to ask, "Have you ever been arrested?" they can inquire, "Have you ever been convicted of a crime?"

Are interviewers walking on eggshells?

The Equal Employment Opportunities Act and other employment laws have certainly placed restrictions on employers.

Are you walking on eggshells?

Even when you know a question is illegal, if you want the job, is it advantageous to stop the interviewer to point out the question is illegal?

FIRST THINGS FIRST

Know the law. You don't have to be an expert but when you know more about what is and isn't permitted, you'll find it easier to maintain composure and decide how to proceed.

◆ Some illegal questions are asked because the employer and the employer's representatives are ignorant of the law.

◆ Some sensitive topics may be introduced when questions are properly phrased.

◆ Some questions are discriminatory and a job seeker can take legal action.

DON'T IGNORE CONCERNS

Interviewers typically want information to help allay concerns. If you can guess why an offensive or illegal question is asked, you'll banish concerns and score points.

Scenario X

Jessica G. knows she's well qualified for the job of Corporate Relocation Consultant in a major moving company. During the interview, she is asked if she's married. This is a no-no question and Jessica knows it but she says, "Yes."

"Is your husband the main wage earner?"

"How would that impact my job performance?" she counters.

"It's our experience the main wage earner's job gets the first consideration if there's a family crisis."

Jessica reasons the concern here is absenteeism.

"I have an excellent attendance record. It's a source of personal pride," she adds. "You can easily check this with my former employer."

Jessica received a job offer.

Scenario Y

John R. is asked what he currently earns. He wants to reply, "That's none of your business!" Instead he asks, "What do insurance adjusters earn in this company?"

The interviewer ignores his question. Later, she comments, "I'll have to see a copy of a payroll stub or a copy of your tax return."

"Why?"

"I can't schedule you for a second interview without information about your current wages."

He assures her, "I can accept standard company wages if you can tell me the company recognizes and rewards hard work."

John's interview was scheduled for the following Monday.

Scenario Z

"Do you own or rent your home?" "What are the ages of your children?" "Do you have a drug or alcohol problem or have you ever had one?" These three prohibited questions were asked when Sam D. sat down with the interviewer at the ABC Company.

"This must be a test of my knowledge of the law," he announced. "All of your questions, so far, are illegal."

Here's what happened next: The interviewer backed down.

In Scenario Z, the interviewer switched gears and asked Sam D. about his management experience. The interviewer may judge Sam to be a direct, no-nonsense person. Many find this an admirable trait for a manager to possess.

Do you think Sam received a job offer?

You'd have to know more about the interviewer to provide a sound answer. The fact is, you won't know more about the person interviewing you. You'll want to consider how you'll respond to such questions before they arise. Another strategy is to ignore the question. You don't want it to appear as though you didn't hear the question so you may want to introduce a new topic.

"I've lived in Rome County all my adult life. I'd be able to drive to customers' stores without asking for directions."

"I supervised three people who were recent college graduates and felt good when one of them was promoted to assistant manager ten months later."

"When the company downsized and my responsibilities doubled, I took a crash course in time management. The course was worth every penny and every minute I spent on it."

CAN THEY DO THAT?

Books that focus on how to handle interview questions abound. If you peruse some of these, opt for the ones with the most recent publication dates especially because new laws and modifications impact what's acceptable and what's not acceptable. The seventh edition of the Martin John Yate book *Great Answers to Tough Interview Questions* includes a "vital discussion on handling illegal interview questions." (Kogan Page, 2008). You're not paranoid if you think some questions on job applications and in interview

---

Note: Be aware that only an expert should give you legal advice. Local and federal laws and interpretations change, and competent legal counsel must be your source of up-to-the-minute information should you require it. You may want to begin with the Equal Employment Opportunity Commission in Washington, D.C. (www.eeoc.gov), at 202-663-4900; or call toll-free 1-800-669-4000 to reach the EEOC office closest to you. If you have a TTY device for the hearing impaired, the number is 1-800-669-6820.

---

sessions are illegal. It follows that once you're hired this kind of problem can persist.

FIRST IMPRESSIONS

First impressions are valuable. If you feel the company in which you're seeking employment has bent, if not broken, the law on the application form, during the interview process, or anywhere along the line, you may find yourself looking for confirmation after you've accepted the job offer.

Arbitrary rules about hair length, beards, or strict dress code, and company rules that stifle your freedom may be rife if you accept a job with this company.

The interviewer(s) aren't the only ones making a decision. You make your decision based on a multitude of factors and you're well advised to include your first impression in the process. If not, the price to pay may be a short term of employment with the company and then you'll be reading this book again! You want to choose well and accept a job offer from a company in which you expect to prosper.

A CAN OF WORMS

If you bring up subject matter the interviewer isn't permitted to discuss, you open a can of worms. Now, the interviewer can easily pursue the topic. Here are some examples.

> *My former husband is a citizen of France and he taught me to speak French.*

The interviewer knows you were divorced. You may be asked, "Did you remarry?" It's no one's business, but how can you object to the question? Go ahead—boast about your facility with a second language but anything more is unproductive.

My youngest child started school this month.

The interviewer knows you have more than one child and that one of the youngsters is about five years old. You may be asked, "How many children do you have?" This information won't tell the interviewer if you can do the job. It shouldn't be asked. But you introduced the subject. Some interviewers may conclude you're a stable individual with family responsibilities. Others may determine you have responsibilities that may keep you from the workplace more often than another job candidate who has older children or doesn't have a family.

It's such a relief to have Mom live with us now. I worried when she was alone.

The interviewer knows you have responsibility for an older relative. That kind of personal information may indicate you're a caring individual but it probably won't help you get a job offer and shouldn't be volunteered; for example, if the job requires that you travel, the interviewer may think you won't be free to do so. Even if your mother is a vital person who helps with childcare and makes it possible for you to go to work without worry, the interviewer isn't likely to have a full picture. Of course, if you think this kind of information can help win a job offer, introduce it.

When my sister became a nun, I decided to teach Sunday school.

It's reasonable to assume you and your sister embrace the same religion. If you have a specific reason to tell the interviewer you teach

Sunday school (such as demonstrating you have teaching experience), say what you mean. There's nothing to be gained by elaborating on your religious beliefs. Of course, if you are interviewing for work in your church, it may be pertinent information to impart.

YES AND NO

> *"Yes," I answered you last night;*
> *"No," this morning, sir, I say:*
> *"Colors seen by candlelight*
> *Will not look the same by day."*

wrote the poet Elizabeth Barrett Browning.

The same response in one setting (as by candlelight) will be wholly inappropriate in another setting (as by day). It will be up to you to make quick decisions based upon whether what you divulge will advance your position or not.

If you remember that potential employers are advised to think in terms of skills needed to perform the job and told to consider your aptitude, temperament, and interests, you're better able to decide how you'll respond.

It's a judgment call—nothing more, nothing less. You don't have sufficient information to know in advance whether you're making a good decision when you cooperate with the interviewer who asks what shouldn't be asked. Be positive. Maneuver as best you can but recognize that your standards of conduct and moral judgment—your moral philosophy—matter to you. When you're feeling pressed to get a job offer, it's tempting to let your guard down. You don't have to do it.

Chapter 10

Electronic Communication: A Part of the Interview Process

◆

"A word fitly spoken is like apples of gold in pictures of silver."

—Proverbs 25:11

The interview went well. The job candidate left the building feeling good. She had the manager's business card tucked into her briefcase and she thought about acting on the invitation, "If you think of further questions, send an e-mail to me. My address is on the card." His mobile phone number was on the business card too along with the URL (Web address) for his blog. She could tell at a glance it was an industry-specific blog.

Now more than ever, electronic tools are a fact of life. At one time, this job candidate may have submitted her résumé using a fax machine. The fax (i.e., facsimile machine) is no longer the only game in town, and today résumés can be sent via e-mail. In some cases, keyword-searchable databases are the first to "see" résumés. Not only must you use e-mail; you'll want to have the appropriate keywords in your résumé so that you're moved forward in the search process. (It's strange how the ancient proverb printed above applies to this modern-day phenomenon.)

No matter whether you send résumés and related documents by fax or e-mail or hand deliver them, be mindful of the words you use. Avoid abbreviations, especially those that may not be widely understood. Job candidates who are accustomed to texting, for example, should overcome the inclination to write *NLT*, which stands for "no later than," or *BME*, "based on my experience"— or any one of the more than one thousand text-messaging abbreviations that are in use today. Use complete sentences and proper grammar when you write. Clear communication helps to avoid misunderstandings. It's risky to compose online, because it takes only the push of a button to send the message on its way. You'll want to be sure you have said what you mean before things are out of your hands.

VIDEO CONFERENCING

If you or people you know have never been through this kind of interview process, it's easy to think it's a figment of the imagination. It's not.

When job candidates are in different geographic locations, video conferencing can be used to screen people and determine who should be supplied with an expense-paid trip to headquarters for an on-site interview.

It's practical for companies that engage in telecommuting or maintain remote or virtual offices to arrange for comprehensive video conferencing interviews so that key players participate. Just as you may be introduced to a recruiter, a hiring manager, and his or her boss if you're on location, in a video conference interview it can be a collaborative effort. If in your mind's eye you see people hurling questions and talking at the same time, or chatting with one another on the side, you may be right!

A video conferencing interview can be grueling. You'll be challenged to project your personality and showcase yourself in a quasi-sterile setting. Yet, a promoter of video conferencing touts benefits, "Body language and other external stimuli help convey a more complete message to participants in a discussion."

IS THE GLASS HALF FULL OR HALF EMPTY?

If you're asked to participate in an electronic interview you had better see the glass as half full.

One way to prepare for any interview, especially a video conference *chat*, is to be at ease as a public speaker. *Boost Your Presentation IQ: Proven Techniques for Winning Presentations and Speeches*, by this author (McGraw-Hill, 2006), explains popular types of presentations, and should start you thinking about the video conference in new and different ways. An organization like Toastmasters International prepares speakers to do well under fire (see Chapter 5).

Focus on the following behavior patterns.

1. *Concentrate.* Don't allow yourself to be distracted. If you can't hear or the sound system squeals, let the interviewer know, then persevere.

2. *Be natural.* Don't exaggerate your body language; don't minimize your movements either.

3. *Make eye contact* with the camera.

4. *Repeat the question* aloud, giving yourself a moment to compose yourself. Skilled public speakers do this when they answer questions. They're so glib you may not have noticed. For example:

> *Mr. Brick wants to know, how many people I supervised at the Latzen Plant.*

> *"What was the greatest challenge I ever faced in the meeting room?" you ask.*

> *Tell about the year I spent working in France.*

5. *Don't hurry.* Pauses and hesitations tend to be amplified in a video conference setting. If you've rehearsed and prepared well for the meeting, this shouldn't be a problem. Be aware, however, there's no need to rush in and fill up silences. If you let the other person speak up, you won't risk saying something you didn't want to say.

If the interviewer appears to be larger than life on the video screen, remind yourself it's a trick of the camera.

At the conclusion of the interview, you may want to remain in the chair. If you rise and walk out of view, the finale may seem abrupt to onlookers. Remember, the session is over when the camera is off.

CAPTURE THE MOMENT

When it comes to interviews and electronic communication, potential employers may take the lead but you can take advantage of these tools, too. Carry a pocket-size recorder with you and make a few remarks immediately following the interview. Or, make notes using your laptop or Blackberry, etc. Immediate response and first impressions are valuable. Important details are often forgotten when you concentrate on a train schedule, or which road leads back to the highway.

It's not likely you picked up the interviewers' business cards, so make sure you know names, proper spelling, and titles so you can send appropriate thank-you letters.

Even though an interview takes place in a rarified setting, standard formalities apply.

Chapter 11

◆

After the Interview: Do's and Don'ts

◆

*"Bodily exercise, when compulsory,
does no harm to the body; but knowledge
which is acquired under compulsion
obtains no hold on the mind."*

—Plato

Most of the chapters in this book deal with reasons why you should or shouldn't take some action. This chapter isn't especially concerned with offering reasons why.

JUST DO IT!

Or, don't—as the case may be.

As to Plato's observation on page 108—your goal is to gain a hold on the minds of those who extend job offers. Accordingly,

JUST DO IT

STEP 1.
Record key points as soon as possible.

Use a tape recorder or notebook. Choose a mode you'll be able to refer to with ease.

Analyze your performance and record anything special about the job or the company that you didn't know beforehand. If during your rehearsal period you discovered a weak point and worked to improve it, be sure to record whether you were successful. Rate your rehearsal, or preparation, too. Hindsight is usually 20/20. Prior to the actual interview, you anticipated questions. Were you correct? Were you well prepared? How did you do?

Scenario A:
A hopeful project manager received a job offer from a publisher. She was excited about the job and a productive future with the company, but when she attempted to negotiate the salary, the publishing executive withdrew the job offer.

The job seeker kept copious notes. Hours after meeting with the publishing executive she wrote in her notes, "Don't feel bad if they won't meet your price. Management doesn't appear to be realistic about what can be accomplished. There will be lots of room for failure. As a result, long hours will be required and you'll be toiling for little remuneration unless there's a dollar compromise." Not only did her notes cause her to approach her next salary negotiation more cautiously, they also helped maintain her self-confidence.

After three months, she received and accepted a fine job offer, and she recognized that her initial reaction wasn't frivolous. It would have been nice to have that job, but it wasn't a good one—under the circumstances. She later learned that the job turned into a revolving door for three project managers who each left the position after 90 days or so with the company.

◆

STEP 2.
Write thank-you note(s).

A short note that has the following components should be mailed within 24 hours of your interview:

1. Say thanks for the time the interviewer extended to you or for explanations provided. Get specific and be sure you focus on something the recipient of the letter actually did to deserve this note.

2. The letter shouldn't be longer than one page. Be scrupulous about using correct spelling, grammar, and punctuation. Take special care with the individual's name and title. If in doubt, call a company representative to check your facts.

3. Etiquette experts tell us that e-mail thank-you notes are permitted. Still, there's nothing distinctive about them, and some recipients find them distasteful. You're not likely to cause any distress by sending a handwritten thank-you note via the postal

service. It's clear to the recipient that you had to take a little more time and care to say thank you, and you did!

4. If more than one thank-you letter is to be written, give each recipient a customized thank you. Be creative and don't repeat whole phrases. There's more than one way to say the same thing.

STEP 3.

Mark your calendar to contact the primary interviewer at some future date, if necessary.

If you were told a decision won't be made for about ten days, your calendar date should reflect that information. A call to a company representative beforehand isn't likely to reveal anything. Even if you receive another job offer while you're waiting, weigh your options with care. If you accept the other position and then get a job offer

from a preferred company, will anything be lost? This is one time you'll probably gain little or nothing by acting instead of reacting.

If you haven't heard anything after the time mentioned, you may want to call to ask if a decision has been made.

Scenario B:

Sharon G. expected to be called back to work at the Wilson Company after July 1. In the meantime, she accepted a temporary position with the Ellison Brothers Furniture Emporium. Jeff Ellison offered her a permanent position contingent upon the opening of a new store in June. Sharon planned to return to the Wilson Company but the June 15 date of the Ellison's store opening preceded the Wilson Company promise of work. She accepted Jeff Ellison's offer and four months later (obviously not as early as originally announced), when a Wilson Company representative finally called with a job offer, she declined.

Although this scenario reflects one person's response to a job offer, it spotlights the fact that the job seeker doesn't control everything. By making decisions on matters within your control you advance your position.

STEP 4.

Prior to any after-the-interview contact with the company, conduct an image checkup.

Many interviewers don't find out if you're a dedicated, sensitive person or how you go about accomplishing tasks. They typically won't know more about you unless you're hired. What you do or don't do after the interview is revealing. Ask yourself, "How would it appear if . . .?" before you take action.

◆ How would it appear if I notified Mr. Cleary his automated voice mail message is difficult to hear?

◆ How would it appear if I sent the receptionist in the Human Resources office a copy of that organic foods article we discussed?

◆ How would it appear if I sent a note with the names of two more personal references since I only filled in one reference on the company's form?

Remember, this is business, not pleasure. If your action isn't likely to enhance your image with key players, don't act!

STEP 5.
Don't accept the offer before you get it.

Or, as the saying goes: Don't count your chickens before they hatch. Rejection is part of the job seeking process. Even when you know the interview went well and were led to believe "this job is yours," it ain't over 'til it's over. Five minutes after you leave the office, management could decide to freeze all hiring plans until the new budget is approved.

Scenario C:
Bob N. was elated about the prospect of working for ReCycle Michael, Inc. He spent the weekend weighing the pros and cons of selling or renting his duplex apartment in order to spend less time commuting by moving to downtown Dayton. He had also had

another interview but he didn't bother writing a thank-you note to Ted Grimes, the Human Resources Vice President at Felding Brothers, because a job with them was obviously a moot point. When Bob was told someone else had been hired for the ReCycle Michael job, he was more than disappointed. He lost productive time while pulling himself out of the doldrums.

◆

STEP 6.
Make plans for learning and growing.

If you've been called in to interview, chances are you meet the job criterion and haven't fooled anyone. Still, if there's a recurring theme during interviews, such as your lack of facility with desktop publishing software or little experience managing people, consider what you should do about it.

It's easy to lose sight of these soft spots once you get a job offer and start working. Since most people expect to work for several different employers during their work career, you might as well take advantage of what you learned during the interview process. Strengthen skills you're not currently able to boast about. Your new position may give you an opportunity to do that, or you may want to return to a classroom, engage in volunteer work, or take other steps necessary to fill in the missing pieces.

STEP 7.
Don't forget to update interested parties.

If a friend or acquaintance gave you a lead and by following it you got an interview, or better still, an offer and job, be sure to let your friend know what transpired. When someone intercedes on your behalf, it's courteous to say "Thanks," but it's downright rude to neglect to inform that person of your progress.

Scenario D:

Marilyn T. approached Hilliard Publishers' management with an offer to provide marketing services. Her friend Gary knew Henry Hilliard and told Marilyn he would probably be amenable to fresh ideas for marketing while he might not listen to much else. When H. H. offered her a job as senior editor she was elated. Editing was her forte while writing marketing copy was a secondary skill. Two weeks after she began to work at Hilliard Publishers she was called into a meeting with some outside vendors. Gary was there. Although Gary congratulated her, she felt their friendship was never quite the same again. Gary may or may not have been annoyed by Marilyn's failure to contact him with the good news, but Marilyn was embarrassed. So the dynamics of the relationship were altered. A small matter? Perhaps. But, one that is easily avoided and unnecessary.

◆

STEP 8.

Reserve judgment when your lips say "Yes" but there's "No-No" in your thoughts.

If you accept a job that offers less than you wanted—less money— less opportunity for growth, less chance to use your skills—adapt a wait-and-see position. You did, after all, say "Yes." Arrive at the job with a positive attitude. Don't compromise your admirable work ethics and do maintain high standards. You wouldn't be the first person to be hired for a position and later transferred to another, more suitable position, or leave with your boss who accepts a job at another company, or . . . the possibilities are endless. It's best to accept a promising job offer, but this isn't a perfect world, so when you accept an offer, focus on the upside. You may eventually decide to start the job hunt process over again. Promise yourself a hiatus from this task for a reasonable period and concentrate on getting acclimated to the new work environment.

Scenario E:

A bricklayer went home each evening exhausted and in a bad mood. The man who worked at his side usually appeared to be content. "This is a backbreaking job," said the first man. "This week's paycheck helps pay my son's college tuition," observed the other man.

Will the two men always be bricklayers? Perhaps.

Will the one man always focus on the negatives? Perhaps.

Will you?

Chapter 12

Resources You Should Know About

*"Human felicity is produced not so much by
great pieces of good fortune that seldom
happen, as by little advantages that occur
everyday."*

—Benjamin Franklin's autobiography

Excellent resources proliferate. Use popular search engines (e.g.,
www.google.com, www.bing.com, www.yahoo.com) to search the
Internet for books and articles that relate to interviews. But don't
stop there. Be creative with the search words you input. For example, "job interviews" comes immediately to mind, but how about

"self-confidence"? Or, "how to handle stress"? "My interview wardrobe"?

Your local library is a good resource. Use it! Browse library shelves and check with librarians. You may want to ask a research librarian to assist you in gathering company-specific information. Even if you're good at gathering information, these specialists are masters of the hunt. Take advantage of their expertise and willingness to help.

Be aware of the source. Just because the topic is in print or online doesn't mean it's accurate or helpful. It may be little more than the writer's opinion, without benefit of any research. If a book or article is old (i.e., six years or more), it's likely to be incomplete. Opt for recently published material. And, don't spend time on materials that tell you sad stories—*Oh, it's tough out there. . . .* You simply don't have time to wallow!

Don't relegate a mentor's ability to assess a situation and provide valuable guidance strictly to on-the-job challenges—rely on it when you're outside, waiting to get in!

1. A *mentor* who is employed by a company you just left is still a mentor. Mentors probably know your strong points and can give you tips for conducting yourself at job interviews to feature your strengths.

2. Do you belong to *business organizations?* In addition to the obvious—networking to discover job openings—you may be able to locate help as you prepare for an interview.

3. Check the *membership roster.* Contact a comember who works for the company you want to work for or who works in the same industry. Explain your interest and ask for background information. This approach may lead to a flood of information you can't find elsewhere. You would be obtaining only one per-

son's opinion, but you may learn something about the corporate culture or some issue that benefits you.

If, for example, the interviewer says, "Tell me a little about yourself," you won't mention the plethora of outside activities you're engaged in if you discovered that top management frowns on anyone spending too much time away from the family after work hours. Legally speaking, that's a nonissue, but why should you volunteer this information?

4. *Over 40 and preparing to interview?* Should you do things differently than anyone else?

According to some experts, you'll want to appear youthful. If that translates into being energetic, willing to embrace new ideas, facility with modern communication systems (such as software programs, paging systems, cellular telephones), who can argue the point?

Still, if you're over 40, 50, or 60, and interviewing, you may *think* you have valid concerns that anyone younger wouldn't have reason to consider. Would it surprise you to learn it's possible to turn those years and experience into an advantage?

5. *Check out articles that accentuate the positive.* Jumpstart Your Job Search has a section for those past the half-century mark (www.jumpstartyourjobsearch.com/over50.html) that is worthy of note. This site leads you to others and contains optimistic news for the over-50 set of job hunters.

U.S. Bureau of Labor Statistics and surveys by private organizations suggest those stories about older workers being "out of the loop" don't hold up.

Some articles suggest that employers actually favor older workers they perceive to be more productive and embracing superior work ethics. Maturity is also considered an asset when you train people or provide counseling, because it *suggests* you're experienced and capable.

6. *Self-confidence is an issue at any age.* If you believe that when the interviewer sees your gray hair and other telltale signs of aging you'll be eliminated from consideration, do what it takes to boost your self-confidence. A new haircut, cosmetic makeover, and regular trips to an exercise center are some of the ways people choose to improve physical appearance and mental well-being.

7. You may want to read *motivational books and listen to tapes* made by some of the gurus of the genre, or you may find *talk-*

ing with a religious leader or personal counselor will help put you on the positive track.

"How to Stay Employable: A Guide for the Mid-life and Older Worker," is published by the American Association of Retired Persons, Washington, D.C.

8. **Warning:** Books with titles that suggest there is a problem can make you *believe* there is a problem—so approach them with caution. Still, when you find good information such as: It may be time for a career change, explore that information with an open mind.

It's easy to treat yourself to *motivational support* by tapping into the Internet. Some Web sites offer to automatically deliver positive messages to your e-mail address without cost to you. Reportedly you can "unsubscribe" at any time. You may want to give one or two of them a try.

◆ www.yourdailymotivation.com

◆ www.greatday.com

◆ www.thedailyguru.com

◆ www.motivational-messages.com

9. Every job seeker preparing for an interview is aided by a good *speaking voice*. A few sessions with a voice coach may help correct rapid speech, the tendency to speak too softly, and other impediments.

10. *Do you have a buddy?* Someone who is a friend and sympathetic listener? Someone whose opinion you respect? Many folks have a relationship with someone who fits that description but they don't think of that person as a buddy. (Think again!)

A mentor is achievement-focused while a buddy's scope of interest is generally broader. Communicate with a buddy often during the job hunt interview period. If you don't have a buddy, look for one. A terrific buddy is a terrific resource!

Your buddy can help keep things in perspective so you find it easier to maintain a positive, upbeat attitude. When laughter frequently spills into conversations you have with your buddy, you're twice blessed.

Chapter 13

A Powerful
Strategy That
Guarantees Success

"Tiny differences in input could quickly become overwhelming differences in output . . .

In weather, for example, this translates into what is only half-jokingly known as the Butterfly Effect—the notion that a butterfly stirring the air today in Peking can transform storm systems next month in New York."

—James Gleick

This final chapter of *Get the Job! Interview Strategies That Work* should be read over and over and over and—well, you get the idea.

That's because it's smart to greet any challenge with an I-can-do-it mentality, but it's an essential approach when you're in pursuit of employment. It's a time when you face some rejection and it's nice to be reminded—I can do it—over and over and . . .

It's also smart to greet any challenge with a healthy dose of realistic expectations. Try to assess factors related to your job search with precision and clarity.

Put the two together:

◆ I can do it—I have the ability and the desire.

◆ This is attainable—I'm in the right place at the right time.

Now, get ready for success.

When you don't consciously examine your preparedness and the likelihood that you'll get the job you want, you *may* get a job offer. But when you're prepared and practical you *will* get a job offer.

Someone must extend the job offer to you but when you believe in yourself and put yourself in the right place at the right time, *you* make it happen. The perception that control is exclusively in the hands of others is the bain of many a job seeker's existence.

Or, as a wise man once said, "You won't see the sunset if you're heading east." Use what you know to get what you want.

PREPARED AND PRACTICAL

An experienced woodchopper searching for work in the barren desert won't find work as a woodchopper. He has the ability and the desire, but he's not in the right place. The woodchopper should enlarge his search area. It's impractical to look for work nearby.

This final chapter is different from earlier chapters that relate strictly to the job interview. It's necessary to broaden the spotlight in order to examine the powerful strategy that guarantees success.

Who are you when you sit in the interview chair?

1. You're someone who can do the job and has the ability and the desire.

2. You're likely to get a job offer because you're in the right place at the right time.

1 + 2 = This result: You've empowered yourself to succeed.

PREPARED

Education, training, years of experience, and certification are some of the factors that support someone's ability to function in a role. There's not always a perfect match for a job description so it follows that there are tradeoffs. You may, for example, have all the needed experience. You may have additional attributes that you recognize will help you to do this job. You may convince the people who do the hiring that you *can do* the job in spite of the fact that you don't have certification. If necessary, you can eventually satisfy requirements to get certification.

The co-message is that you *want to* do the job.

Inner doubts can easily sabotage a job seeker's presentation.

The woodchopper, for example, may be so happy living in the desert he doesn't want to move away. When he attempts to convince the person who is hiring woodchoppers in a neighboring state that he's the man for the job, he's not convincing about wanting the job—probably because he's not convinced himself.

If the woodchopper decided to move away from the desert so he could earn a living while he prepared for a career that offered gainful employment in the desert, he might feel differently. He'd look upon this out-of-town job as a means to an end and want to be hired.

He'd combine steps one and two and empower himself to succeed.

You're probably not looking for gainful employment as a wood-chopper in a tree-free desert. You can, however, apply the same analysis to your job search. Get specific. Ask yourself whether

1. you're someone who can do the job, has the ability and the desire.

2. you're likely to get a job offer because you're in the right place at the right time.

Say Yes. Believe Yes. You empower yourself to succeed.

PRACTICAL

Let's view James Gleick's observation at the beginning of this chapter from another perspective, "Tiny differences in input could quickly become overwhelming differences in output." When you're involved in a job search you should be in tiptop condition; yet, it's a time when you may be so focused on needing a job that you let other needs go. You need

◆ good nutrition.

◆ exercise.

◆ peace and serenity.

If tiny differences translate into lapses in good nutrition, exercise, peace and serenity, and other things you need to function well, you're likely to experience dramatic differences in output.

If you're practical, you'll be attentive to keeping yourself in top condition, not because your mother told you to do so, or because it's what conventional wisdom dictates, but because when you're good to yourself, you maintain self-confidence and you're better prepared to achieve goals.

There is something magical about self-confidence.
Men and women who exhibit it attract more than

> *their share of attention from others, and they*
> *advance further and faster in their careers. They*
> *somehow seem to have been born under a different*
> *star. Success comes to them easily and naturally.*

These words appear in the Planning Ahead: Job Tips section in the January 27, 1997 issue of *Federal Times,* (Army Times Publishing). The writer goes on to say that self-confidence can be mastered and gives a list of tips. The writer attributes these observations to a book by Samuel A. Cypert, *The Power of Self-Esteem,* (Amacom, 1994).

This is not a revolutionary concept but it needs the spotlight now because you need to sustain the I-can-do-it mentality.

GOOD NEWS

The good news is that it's not difficult to stay in top condition, and if you master the process now, it's yours forever. It's not only a tool you'll use to prepare to ace a job interview, it's an asset you'll add to your personal repertoire so you'll ace life!

Because job search times are not the easiest of times, keep yourself in tiptop condition now and you'll easily be able to keep yourself in tiptop condition anytime, anywhere.

TALK TO YOURSELF

You may be an outgoing individual who engages strangers in conversation as readily as you do close friends, or you may be a classic introvert. In either case, you talk to yourself. Virtually everyone does. You converse with an inner voice.

◆ You're in over your head.

◆ You're not going to win.

◆ If you try, you'll make a fool of yourself.

If messages like these sound familiar, you've been conversing with an inner voice that delivers negative messages.

You are the one on both sides of the conversation, and you can change the dialogue.

◆ This challenge is a great opportunity.

◆ I've got an excellent chance of winning.

◆ I'll feel good if I try.

When you train your inner voice to deliver positive feedback, you're taking another practical step towards boosting your I-can-do-it mentality.

Notice, the positive comments aren't fabrications. You don't want to prime your inner voice to lie because you won't believe the message. You've got to believe! The assertions offer a fresh, useful approach to assessing your position. It's better to be positive because positive reinforcement energizes you, and energy and enthusiasm help take you where you want to go.

If you're not immediately able to turn negative messages around, tune them out. Stories abound that tell about people who reprogrammed their inner critics and moved forward to achieve goals. Read these stories. You'll find them in popular magazines, newspapers, and in books at the library and bookstore. Biographies of famous people, for example, often reveal hardships they overcame to achieve fame and fortune. You may hear stories about people who turned fear into success when you attend services at your place of worship. Motivational seminars and tapes are filled with examples that illustrate how a positive way of approaching challenges enables people to succeed.

The most important revelation may be your awareness that when you talk to yourself, you're less than kind. Be a friend to yourself.

Speaking of friends, *spend more time with positive people*. The laughter and optimistic views positive people project put you in the mood to do the same while doomsday people tend to suck the air out of the room and leave you deflated.

Make lists. Mark off your achievements. It's another way to validate your status as a capable I-can-do-it person.

Football Coach Lou Holtz reportedly maintained a list of personal goals that at one time numbered more than one hundred. He achieved many of the goals—such as parachuting out of an airplane, getting a hole in one—and the list served as a visible reminder of progress. As some goals were achieved, new ones were added to the list.

Such a list has a life of its own. If this technique appeals to you, start your own list. Use whatever methods you wish in order to keep yourself on a positive track.

Positive thought gives rise to positive self-talk and vice versa.

It's practical to conclude that since you talk to yourself, anyway, you might as well make the conversation constructive.

ABILITY AND DESIRE CHECKLIST

Take a bow—you've been invited for an interview. Now, all you've got to do is convince the interviewer(s) that you're the person they think you are.

1. Today's business environment changes rapidly and you may need to fine-tune some of your skills; for example, if you want a job in corporate communications, you may have to operate desktop publishing software. Do you? No matter what your area of expertise, are you up to the minute in state-of-the-art skills?

   YES......... NO..........

2. If a job you want is in a big city and you think of yourself as a small-town kind of person, or if the job is in a small town and you're accustomed to life in the city, are you prepared to move?

Is your spouse ready to move? How will this move affect your children? No matter whether you're single or married with kids, a long-distance move causes upheaval in your personal life. Do the benefits outweigh what may be considered an impact on your quality of life? Are you prepared for transition?

YES......... NO..........

3. You've been self-employed for years, or worked for a company but had a good deal of independence. The position you want is more of a team-effort position. You'll have to interact with others more closely. Or it may be the reverse; you're accustomed to working with others and not doing it alone. When the interviewer asks why you want to give up the work environment in which you currently operate, can you speak intelligently about the pros and cons of each? Are you convinced this new way will suit you better? YES......... NO..........

4. You've worked in promotions for a small company and can document your success with numbers demonstrating the company's growth. Now you want to do this work for a large company. Have you considered whether your skills translate to the new environment and new demands? Are you asking for the wrong position? Should you be seeking a job as an assistant director instead of director? Assistant editor instead of editor-in-chief? Can you do the job? Of course, people take giant steps up the ladder of success. Do you recognize there will be a period of adjustment? YES......... NO..........

If you answer YES to most of these questions, you've empowered yourself to succeed. If you hesitate before you answer, or find yourself replying in the negative, it's probably time to rethink your strategy. You want job offers. All the rest is fiddle-faddle!

INDEX